MW00325229

BAPTISM

WHAT THE BIBLE TEACHES

TONY TWIST, PH.D., D.MIN.
BOBBY HARRINGTON, D.MIN.
& DAVID YOUNG PH.D.

Baptism: What the Bible Really Teaches
Copyright © 2018 by Tony Twist, Bobby Harrington, and David Young

Distributed by Renew, a network that renews the teachings of Jesus to fuel disciple making. We are a multi-ethnic, multi-national, and multi-generational community, equipping millions of disciples and disciple makers.

All Scripture quotations, unless otherwise indicated, are taken from the Holy Bible, New International Version®, NIV®. Copyright ©1973, 1978, 1984 by Biblica, Inc.™ Used by permission of Zondervan. All rights reserved worldwide. www.zondervan.com The "NIV" and "New International Version" are trademarks registered in the United States Patent and Trademark Office by Biblica, Inc.™

All emphases in Scripture quotations and other quotations are from the authors.

Any Internet addresses (websites, blogs, etc.) in this book are offered as a resource. They are not intended in any way to be or imply an endorsement by Renew.org. Nor does Renew.org vouch for the content of these addresses for the life of this eBook.

ISBN: 978-1-949921-02-1

Cover and interior design: Harrington Interactive Media

To Joanne, Gerald, Don, Nancy, and Bob
for your encouragement for the ministry of Renew

CONTENTS

CHAPTER 11. The Timing of Baptism

RENƎW

RENEWING THE TEACHINGS OF JESUS
TO FUEL DISCIPLE MAKING

RENEW.ORG

AUTHOR BIOGRAPHIES

TONY TWIST is the President and CEO of the TCM International Institute, a global seminary and graduate school for disciple makers based in both Indianapolis, Indiana, and Heiligenkreuz, Austria. His formal education included Milligan College, Emmanuel Christian Seminary, Southern Baptist Seminary (D. Min.), and Indiana University (Ph.D.). Tony grew up in Dallas, Texas and Alice Springs, N.T., Australia. Following graduation from Milligan he married Suzanne Grogan from Spencer, Virginia. He and Suzanne served churches in Virginia, Tennessee, and Indiana with a primary focus on disciple making. His passions are disciple making, spending time with Suzanne, working out, and making new friends around the world. Tony is a co-founder of Renew.

DAVID YOUNG completed an M.A. at Harding School of Theology and an M.A. and Ph.D. in New Testament at Vanderbilt University. He has worked for churches in Missouri, Kansas, and Tennessee, taught at several universities, and spoken around the world. He is the host of the New Day Television Program and author of several books, including *The Rhetoric of Jesus in the Gospel of Mark* (Fortress Press, 2017), based upon his Ph.D. dissertation. David currently serves as the senior minister for the North Boulevard Church of Christ in Murfreesboro, Tennessee. David and his wife Julie have two married children. David is a co-founder of Renew.

BOBBY HARRINGTON has completed graduate work in diverse places like the University of Calgary, Princeton Seminary, and Regent College (Vancouver, Canada). He also holds a D.Min. from Southern Baptist Theological Seminary. He is the founding and current lead pastor of Harpeth Christian Church (by the Harpeth River outside Nashville), the former director of research and development in missional leadership for Stadia, a co-founder of the Relational Discipleship Network, and the co-founder and executive director of discipleship.org. He is also the author or co-author of over ten books on disciple making, including the popular *DiscipleShift* and *The Disciple Makers Handbook*. He is married to Cindy, with two married children and two grandchildren. He is a co-founder and the Executive Director of Renew.

INTRODUCTION

The Core Issues

In recent decades, a disciple-making movement has been sweeping across Western Africa. Men and women who have found amazing joy in following Jesus are leading this movement, and entire villages are turning their lives over to Christ. Many are leaving their animist traditions behind. But some are even leaving the Muslim faith, finding answers in Jesus that they could not find in Islam. One recent image shows seventy Muslim imams lined up at a river in West Africa waiting their turn to be baptized into Jesus Christ. North Americans usually take baptism seriously, but for these imams, the decision to be baptized had life-and-death implications. These imams fully understood that their baptisms signaled a complete break with their past, a safety risk in their future, and most importantly, a new joy in their present. They were eager to express, in the rich symbol of baptism, their joyful allegiance to Jesus Christ. With great courage and faith, they were eager to be born again. For them baptism was the end of one life and the beginning of another.

Water baptism is an age-old symbol of renewal, so it shouldn't surprise us to find it figuring prominently in Scripture, the Christian creeds, or numerous theological works. It is important because it is a practice for most Christian denominations, fellowships, and churches. We have written this book to survey what we believe God's Word teaches about this topic. We are also leaders for the Renew Network, which is made up of men and women from different ecclesial, ethnic, and national backgrounds who seek to follow Jesus Christ as their Lord by following what God's Word teaches.

As we formed Renew, we worked together with others and wrote down our beliefs about the essential and important elements of the Christian faith. We included our beliefs about baptism in a statement on conversion. Simply put, we believe the Bible teaches the following:

> Conversion: God so loved the world that he gave his one and only Son, that whoever believes in him shall not perish but have eternal life. To believe in Jesus means we trust and follow him as both Savior and Lord. When we commit to trust and follow Jesus, we express this faith by repenting from sin, confessing his name, and receiving baptism by immersion in water for the remission of sins. We uphold baptism as the normative means of entry into the life of discipleship. It marks our commitment to regularly die to ourselves and rise to live for Christ in the power of the Holy Spirit. We believe God sovereignly saves as he sees fit, but we are bound by Scripture to uphold this teaching about surrendering to Jesus in faith through repentance, confession, and baptism.

This paragraph was composed and agreed upon after in-depth prayer, reflection, and discussion by the Renew leadership team, including Christian scholars and pastors. This book is a longer exposition that provides the biblical background for our summary statement. We hope it will be helpful for you to know the theology undergirding our call for renewal on the role of baptism in conversion. Our mission is to renew the teachings of Jesus for disciples and disciple makers.

Many people just follow their tradition on this topic or listen to a preacher or a priest, simply accepting what they say. We think a better approach is to continue to listen to those you respect, yes, but also to study God's Word for yourself. Everyday people can know the teachings of Jesus on important issues like baptism. His teachings will bring you renewal, and this renewal will honor God and bring life to you, whoever you are, wherever you live, and whatever you do.

* * *

We believe that salvation and right relationship with God are "by grace through faith in Jesus Christ" (Eph. 2:8-9). This statement gets to the heart of what the Bible teaches about our relationship with God. We emphasize this core teaching, and we also believe our relationship with God is intimately tied to baptism in the Bible. We generally see baptism as the point at which we seal our decision to repent, place our faith in Jesus Christ, commit ourselves to the path of discipleship, and receive God's forgiveness and the indwelling gift of the Holy Spirit.

Baptism is a difficult topic among believers and disciples around the world. We must prayerfully acknowledge this fact as we begin. So you may want to start with a short prayer and ask God to help you open your heart to hear the Word of God in an open, fresh way. With that same prayerful spirit, read through the following ten passages like it's the first time you have ever read them.

> John 3:5: Jesus answered, "Very truly I tell you, no one can enter the kingdom of God unless they are born of water and the Spirit."

> Matthew 28:19-20: Therefore go and make disciples of all nations, baptizing them in the name of the Father and of the Son and of the Holy Spirit, and teaching them to obey everything I have commanded you. And surely I am with you always, to the very end of the age.

> Acts 2:38: Peter replied, "Repent and be baptized, every one of you, in the name of Jesus Christ for the forgiveness of your sins. And you will receive the gift of the Holy Spirit."

> Acts 16:31-33: They replied, "Believe in the Lord Jesus, and you will be saved—you and your household." Then they spoke

the word of the Lord to him and to all the others in his house. At that hour of the night the jailer took them and washed their wounds; then immediately he and all his household were baptized.

Acts 22:16: And now what are you waiting for? Get up, be baptized and wash your sins away, calling on his name.

Romans 6:3-4: Or don't you know that all of us who were baptized into Christ Jesus were baptized into his death? We were therefore buried with him through baptism into death in order that, just as Christ was raised from the dead through the glory of the Father, we too may live a new life.

Galatians 3:26-27: So in Christ Jesus you are all children of God through faith, for all of you who were baptized into Christ have clothed yourselves with Christ.

Colossians 2:11-12: In him you were also circumcised with a circumcision not performed by human hands. Your whole self ruled by the flesh was put off when you were circumcised by Christ, having been buried with him in baptism, in which you were also raised with him through your faith in the working of God, who raised him from the dead.

Titus 3:4-6: But when the kindness and love of God our Savior appeared, he saved us, not because of righteous things we had done, but because of his mercy. He saved us through the washing of rebirth and renewal by the Holy Spirit, whom he poured out on us generously through Jesus Christ our Savior.

1 Peter 3:21-22: This water [Noah's] symbolizes baptism that now saves you also—not the removal of dirt from the body but the pledge of a clear conscience toward God. It saves you by the resurrection of Jesus Christ, who has gone into heaven and is at God's right hand—with angels, authorities and powers in submission to him.

This short book represents our best thinking and practice, which we also believe is the position given in the Bible for wholesome discipleship and church life.[1] As we demonstrate below, we believe the Word of God teaches that baptism—as an expression of faith—is for the *remission of sins*. This is based upon the exact words of Acts 2:38, it is what the Christians in the earliest period after the apostles believed, and it is reflected in the Nicene Creed of the late 300s.[2] We commend all who will read what we write with an open mind and with a heart that is committed to God's biblical truth as the ultimate standard.

CHAPTER 1

The Appeal of Baptism
Salvation is by the Grace of God Through Jesus Christ

I (Bobby) met Larry, who had lots of questions about the Bible. He started attending church because his son was playing hockey with other teens, and they all attended the same church. At first, Larry came to church just to "check it out." Then, he started regularly attending services. Eventually, he moved from just attending church services on Sundays to joining a small group Bible study during the week. He was in his late fifties, but he had never studied the Bible before. That meant he was confused about various things. This confusion surfaced while he was purchasing a car one day. Larry was talking about church with the car salesman, and the salesman was intrigued by Larry's descriptions of his experiences at church.

"He kept asking me questions about what the church believed," Larry said. "I tried to answer his questions, but I think I gave him every answer except the right one." Then he asked me, "Can you help me, and give me a short description of what Christianity is all about?"

That was a good question, and it led to an engaging conversation. If we had to summarize it all, we would say that true Christianity is about Jesus and the gospel (John 3:16; 1 Cor. 15:1-8). At Renew, we summarize the gospel in the following words:

The Good News is that God sent his one and only Son, Jesus the Messiah to save us. Jesus became one of us, taught us how to live, and then...

- He died on the cross for our sins,

- He was buried,

- He rose on the third day, according to the Scriptures, and appeared to many witnesses.

- He then ascended into heaven and sent his Spirit.

Jesus has been enthroned as King of kings and Lord of lords.

- He is coming back to judge the living and the dead.

- But he first invites everyone into his kingdom, where, by this gospel of grace, we are forgiven, made blameless, and empowered for a new life in this world and in the next.

We respond to the gospel by faith, which means we trust and follow Jesus as his disciples in all things.[3]

We respond to the gospel and express our decision to place faith in Jesus through repentance, confession, and baptism. God meets us at the point of our faith by giving us the forgiveness of sins and the gift of the Holy Spirit.

This salvation is offered as an act of *grace*, the free gift of God through Jesus. All human beings are bankrupt sinners who have nothing we can give God that would gain his favor, and God's freely offered salvation is our only hope. This gift is called grace—often defined as the unearned favor given by God through Jesus Christ's sacrifice for our sins. The wonderful opportunity of salvation "by grace" simply means this: God takes away our sin, breaks Satan's hold on our life, and gives us eternal life through Jesus and his work on the cross, never through our own works.

The following Scripture passages form the foundation for this belief:

Ephesians 2:4-5: But because of his great love for us, God, who is rich in mercy, made us alive with Christ even when we were dead in transgressions—it is by grace you have been saved.

2 Timothy 1:8-10: So do not be ashamed to testify about our Lord. . . who has saved us and called us to a holy life—not because of anything we have done but because of his own purpose and grace. This grace was given us in Christ Jesus before the beginning of time, but it has now been revealed through the appearing of our Savior, Christ Jesus, who has destroyed death and has brought life and immortality to light through the gospel.

Titus 3:4-7: But when the kindness and love of God our savior appeared, he saved us, not because of righteous things we had done, but because of his mercy. . . so that, having been justified by his grace, we might become heirs having the hope of eternal life.

Romans 5:6-8: You see, at just the right time, when we were still powerless, Christ died for the ungodly. Very rarely will anyone die for a righteous man, though for a good man someone might possibly dare to die. But God demonstrates his own love for us in this: While we were still sinners, Christ died for us.

This last passage encapsulates the apostle Paul's entire argument in the first half of Romans. God inspires Paul to show us that every human is utterly in need of God's grace. We cannot do anything to make ourselves right with God or to gain salvation.

Under grace, God does not treat us as we deserve. Instead, he shows us infinite love and mercy. All praise and glory belong to God. Salvation is God's gift; it is a reflection of God's character, and above all, his love for us.

CHAPTER 2

The Heart of Baptism

Salvation is Given to Those Who Place Their Faith in Jesus Christ

It is a strange thing how every year many people in North America have money that has been given to them as an inheritance, but they never claim it. Take for example a recent newspaper article from Ohio, which describes how one man left his heirs half a million dollars and another women left her heirs more than one-hundred eight thousand dollars.[4] The article describes how a financial expert set up an easy-to-use and searchable database just to help people in Ohio find out if they had inheritance gifts waiting for them. It is tragic that many people will never know they had a great gift waiting for them. All they have to do is accept it.

We believe it is even more tragic that many people do not know about the gift that has been offered to them through Jesus Christ. God's Word teaches that salvation is free, but it must be accepted. It is only granted to those who place their faith in Jesus.

We must respond to the gospel. The English words *belief* and *faith* come from the same Greek word in the Bible. We must believe or place our faith in Jesus Christ. God initiates and draws us to place our faith in Jesus, but unfortunately, many resist God's Spirit (Acts 7:51; 1 John 2:20, 27).[5] We must say yes to the Spirit and turn to God by faith in Jesus.

Faith is not meritorious, but it is the channel through which we cling to the one who has merit—God's son, Jesus Christ. Christ's death for our sins is the foundation upon which God, in full harmony with his holiness, offers salvation to those who will trust in Christ. Thus, the Bible teaches that salvation is by grace *through* faith, which is synonymous with belief.

The following scripture passages form the foundation for this belief:

Ephesians 2:8-9: For it is by grace you have been saved, through faith—and this not from yourselves, it is the gift of God—not by works, so that no one can boast.

John 3:16: For God so loved the world that he gave his one and only son, that whoever believes in him shall not perish but have eternal life.

2 Corinthians 5:18-21: All this is from God, who reconciled us to himself through Christ and gave us the ministry of reconciliation: that God was reconciling the world to himself in Christ, not counting people's sins against them… God made him who had no sin to be sin for us, so that in him we might become the righteousness of God.

Thus, while stressing that the only merit that saves us is the merit of Christ, it is necessary to point out that salvation is received through faith.

Faith starts as a decision to rely not just on the gospel of Christ, but also on the person of Christ. Faith inherently carries within it a willingness to obey and a preparedness to act. The Bible teaches that even the demons believe—and shudder (Jam. 2:19). So faith is more than mere mental assent. Indeed, the Greek term for "faith" means something like surrender, loyalty, and allegiance, not just inward acceptance or belief.[6] By surrendering or swearing allegiance, we entrust ourselves to God through Christ and pledge our whole beings and lives to the leadership (i.e., lordship) of Jesus. We embrace Jesus Christ as our leader, teacher, and master.

The initial decision is quite simple; faith is the pledge of our hearts to trust and follow in Jesus. The following passage teaches what is involved in salvation and describes a confession usually made as a statement of faith at one's baptism ceremony:[7]

Romans 10:8-11: The word is near you; it is in your mouth and in your heart, that is, the word of faith we are proclaiming: That if you confess with your mouth, "Jesus is Lord," and believe in your heart that God raised him from the dead, you will be saved. For it is with your heart that you believe and are justified, and it is with your mouth that you confess and are saved. As the scripture says, "Anyone who trusts in him will never be put to shame."

A right standing with God is grounded in a simple faith and a simple confession, which leads into a transforming relationship with God based on trusting and following Jesus Christ.

We have a choice to make when it comes to Jesus Christ. God leads us to himself, as he woos us to Jesus and his gospel by his Spirit. But we must decide to believe. We must make the decision to place our faith in Jesus Christ and accept all that God offers to us through him. Baptism is central because it is the method by which we express this decision to God.

CHAPTER 3

The Purpose of Baptism

Baptism Expresses Faith in Jesus Christ for the Forgiveness of Sins

Bill and Sue are in love, but they are not yet married. They have talked about the commitment and have been together for a long time. In fact, it's been so long since they got together that they act like husband and wife. But they will technically not be married until they pledge their faith to each other with vows and some sort of ceremony. Their faith in and love for each other is the most crucial element in the relationship, but the ceremony is necessary for them to formally commit to a marriage so they can make the relationship officially permanent. In both the eyes of God and those of the state, the wedding ceremony establishes a new relationship, grounded in commitment.

In a like manner, many people are drawn to Jesus and his gospel. They believe in much of what the Bible says, and they do many things that make them seem just like those who are Christians. But like with marriage, they need to express their faith in Jesus through a formal commitment by pledging their faith in Jesus and having a ceremony through which they concretely rely on Jesus and his gospel. That's when their forgiveness of sins is sealed.

In the book, *Hard Sayings of the Bible*, Kaiser and the other authors nicely summarize how this matter was understood in biblical times. The authors use the marriage ceremony analogy, too:

> The normal point of salvation for Christians in the early church was baptism. Even here it is not the ritual itself or the water that saves, but the commitment that one makes to Jesus as Lord... salvation is a relationship. Baptism in Christianity,

just as a wedding in marriage, is simply the way of entering into that relationship.[8]

In this way, we see that baptism is like the disciple's wedding ceremony. As wedding ceremonies make marriage concrete, so does repentance-confession-baptism seal and holistically solidify our relationship with Christ and his forgiveness.

Too often people "accept Christ" by simply giving mental assent or expressing a superficial trust that Jesus died on the cross for their sins. Such a commitment can be shallow and can fail to involve the whole person. Unlike a private mental commitment—or something like it—when you make the conscious decision to repent, verbally confess your faith, and surrender your will to Christ in the ceremony of baptism, the commitment is more all-encompassing and final than merely saying the right thing about Jesus. The washing with physical water signifies the washing away of sins; it is both physical and spiritual reality.

In the same way, as a wedding ceremony solidifies the commitment between husband and wife, baptism solidifies our acceptance of God's grace and our new relationship with him. We summarize the analogy in this way: the ceremony is important, but the heart commitments in the ceremony are of the utmost importance. Baptism is the ceremony; God's forgiveness and our faith in Jesus are the reason for the ceremony.

Baptism, not as a work or an act of merit but as the God-ordained mode of concretely expressing faith in Jesus, is the path we find in God's Word. The following passages give us insight into how baptism connects us to the forgiveness of sins, as we express our faith in Jesus:

Acts 2:37-38: When the people heard this, they were cut to the heart and said to Peter and the other apostles, "Brothers, what shall we do?" Peter replied, "Repent and be baptized, every one of you, *in the name of Jesus Christ for the forgiveness of your sins.* And you will receive the gift of the Holy Spirit."

Acts 22:14-16: Then he said: "The God of our fathers has chosen you to know his will and to see the righteous one and to hear words from his mouth… And now what are you waiting for? Get up, *be baptized and wash your sins away, calling on his name.*"

1 Peter 3:20-22: God waited patiently in the days of Noah while the ark was being built. In it only a few people, eight in all, were saved through water, and this water symbolizes *baptism that now saves you also—not the removal of dirt from the body but the pledge of a good conscience toward God.* It saves you by the resurrection of Jesus Christ, who has gone into heaven and is at God's right hand—with angels, authorities and powers in submission to him.

Each of these passages makes baptism God's method of expressing faith in Jesus to receive the forgiveness of sins and salvation.

In Acts 2:37-38, Peter told the people to be baptized "in the name of Jesus Christ for the forgiveness of your sins." Contrary to what some popular preachers say, this verse does not say that we are baptized because we are forgiven (something that happened before baptism). Those who make this claim often take the English word "for" and make it say we were baptized "for" (meaning "because of") our sins have already been forgiven. This does not work with the Greek text. Instead, the linguistic construction clearly states that baptism puts a person into the state of the forgiveness of their sins. Baptism is "instrumental," meaning that when our baptism expresses our faith in Jesus, it results in the forgiveness of sins.[9]

Each of these passages shows that for the early Christians, baptism was the God-given way to express one's faith commitment to trust and follow Jesus Christ and enter into God's kingdom (John 3:3-5). This is what the earliest Christians believed in the period just after the Bible was written and for hundreds of years after that time. They were taught by the apostles and knew the language in which these passages were written.[10]

Many Evangelical churches do not follow what these passages teach. Instead they encourage people to receive Jesus as Lord and Savior through saying a prayer. In this prayer, people invite Jesus to come into their hearts. Some call it "asking Jesus into your heart" or saying "the sinner's prayer." We are concerned with the tendency of the sinner's prayer to replace baptism as the God-given method for expressing saving faith and how it impacts a person's understanding of conversion and forgiveness.

The idea of just saying a prayer for salvation cannot be found in the Bible (more on this in chapter nine below), but we are even more concerned that this approach too often leads to a shallow, transactional understanding of conversion.[11] A person thinks, *God will forgive my sins if I will just stop and say a brief prayer and accept Christ.* Many people have been led to believe that if they pause from their sinful life for a few moments to offer the sinner's prayer, they receive salvation—even without repentance or a commitment to live a life of faith afterward. This is a problem because this type of faith does not save people. This is part of the reason why more and more evangelical leaders are calling for people to stop this practice, including respected pastors like J.D. Greear, President of the Southern Baptism Convention, who wrote a book called, *Stop Asking Jesus into Your Heart.*[12]

In the chapters below, we hope to show a better way. We believe the better way will become clearer as we explore what God's Word teaches us about baptism—as an expression of our faith—that it is for the remission of sins, just like the early Christians believed, as stated in the passages above and in the Nicene Creed of 381 A.D:[13]

I believe in one God the Father Almighty,
Maker of heaven and earth,
and of all the things visible and invisible…

I acknowledge one baptism for the remission of sins,
and I look for the resurrection of the dead
and the life of the world to come.
Amen.

CHAPTER 4

The Focus of Baptism
Biblical Baptism Emphasizes Jesus Christ and His Gospel

S ome people might think we are teaching that the act of baptism saves a person. Neither the act of baptism nor the waters of baptism are the basis for our forgiveness. We are not saved by what we do. We can only be saved by what Jesus Christ has done for us.

A friend of mine (Bobby) recently said, "I just don't want people to think I believe in baptismal regeneration." This person had been reflecting on the passages we have been looking at and the teachings of this book. He was a well-known Christian leader who has written many books on discipleship, but he had never carefully and fully explored all the passages in the Bible on baptism. "I have come to see that what you are saying is what the Bible teaches, but I do not want to be misunderstood." We think he identified something very important for us to clarify for our readers. Like our friend, we do not want people to think we believe in baptismal regeneration.

What is baptismal regeneration?

It is the view that the act of baptism saves a person. In theological jargon, this means that baptism is the *instrumental cause* of regeneration. Roman Catholic theologians sometimes use the Latin phrase *ex opere operato* (meaning "by the work worked") to describe it. Baptismal regeneration is official doctrine in the Roman Catholic Church. It means that the act of baptism saves a person; it even saves a baby who is not capable of having faith in Jesus.[14] We have great respect for much of what Roman Catholics hold to and practice, but we are convinced that their beliefs and traditions on this matter are not what the Bible teaches.

The Bible teaches that we are saved by grace through faith (Eph. 2:8-9), as we pointed out above. So the ground, or basis, of salvation is God's grace, and we receive it by faith. We are saved by the gospel—what God has done for us through Jesus. We receive this grace and this gospel by faith. Without faith, there is no salvation. If the physical act of baptism *apart from faith* is the basis of salvation, then salvation would be by works, not by faith.

Please carefully note our words: biblical baptism was given to us by God to express our faith in Jesus Christ and his gospel. But the saving power, according to the Bible, is Jesus himself. Our faith relies on Jesus alone (and his saving power). Baptism is only effective because it is God's method of expressing our faith. It will be helpful to review the following passages on this point:

Galatians 3:16-26: So in Christ Jesus you are all children of God *through faith, for all of you who were baptized* into Christ have clothed yourselves with Christ.

Colossians 2:12: ... having been buried with him in *baptism, in which you were also raised with him through your faith* in the working of God, who raised him from the dead.

Acts 22:16: And now what are you waiting for? Get up, be baptized and *wash your sins away, calling on his name.*

Notice how each of these passages describes baptism as an expression of faith.

This is why Jesus said, "He who believes and is baptized will be saved" (Mark 16:16). By baptism people reach out in faith to accept what God provided through Christ. Baptism is about expressing faith in *the name of Jesus.* The phrase "in the name of Jesus Christ" in Acts 2:37-38 and elsewhere is a pledge to rely on Jesus Christ for the forgiveness of sins:

When the people heard this, they were cut to the heart and said to Peter and the other apostles, "Brothers, what shall we do?" Peter replied, "Repent and be baptized, every one of you, *in the name of Jesus Christ for the forgiveness of your sins.* And you will receive the gift of the Holy Spirit."

I. Howard Marshall tells us how we should understand this passage: "However precisely the phrase be understood, it conveys the thought that the person being baptized enters into allegiance to Jesus…. Thus Christian baptism was an expression of faith and commitment to Jesus as Lord."[15]

We see a similar point made in Acts 22:16.[16] This passage summarizes what Ananias told Paul to do in order to be saved by God. After he told Paul about God's mission for him as an apostle, he told Paul to respond by rising up and being baptized to wash away his sins. His baptism was God's prescribed way *to call upon Jesus' name for forgiveness.* These are all different ways of describing baptism as the acceptance of Jesus and commitment to him by faith.

In 1 Peter, the Apostle Peter was encouraging Christians to be faithful to God, even though they were few in number. Peter reminded them of Noah, who was a godly man and one of only a few people (eight in all) that God saved at the time of the flood. Peter said Noah was saved through the waters of the flood, which serves as a foreshadowing of Christian baptism. The water that Noah came through separated him from those who were lost (they drowned and remained alienated from God).

In a similar fashion for Peter's first-century audience, the waters of baptism separated the saved from the unsaved:

Baptism now saves you also—not the removal of dirt from the body but *the pledge of a good conscience toward God. It saves you by the resurrection of Jesus Christ* who has gone into heaven and is at God's right hand—with angels, authorities and powers in submission to him. (1 Peter 3:21, 22)

So baptism divided the saved from the lost. Again, this passage shows the real focus of baptism, which is found not in the act itself, but in the appeal to the resurrection and power of Jesus Christ. Baptism, according to Peter, points to the risen Lord who has angels, authorities, and powers in submission to him. The water of baptism, or the act of baptism, has no merit in itself; it is simply the God-ordained method of appealing by faith to the saving work of Jesus Christ. Baptism, Peter teaches, *is a pledge of a good conscience based upon the resurrection of Jesus Christ.* Baptism, not as a work, but as the expression of saving faith, is what we see taught in the Word of God.

We summarize our point in this way: the ceremony is important, but the underlying elements in the ceremony are the most important. Our faith in Jesus Christ and our forgiveness and new life through him are the reason for the ceremony.

CHAPTER 5

The Repentance of Baptism

Biblical Baptism Expresses Repentance, the Commitment to Turn from Sinful Ways

On the first day of fourth grade, I (Bobby) met Kevin in my classroom. We played football together at recess and soon became fast friends. We loved playing football and hockey together, and we'd go on adventures throughout the city. By the time we were in high school, we would go on double dates with various girls we met, and we got the reputation for dating around. While I went on lots of dates before I met my wife—which was very common at the time—my wife became my only love once we were married. I met Cindy during my second year of University, and we soon fell in love and settled down together—only thirteen months from our first date!

When you get married, you stop dating and commit yourself to one person. Bobby made that commitment, but Kevin didn't. He continued to be known as a ladies' man, going from one relationship to another. He spent time with lots of women over the years. In fact, he dated different women until he was in his mid-fifties. Only then did he finally settled down and commit himself to one lady.

It can be hard for some people to settle down and commit themselves in marriage to one person. But until a person does that, they shouldn't get married. It is a commitment to turn away from all others and devote yourself to the one person you will love forever.

The commitment we have to trust and follow Jesus through baptism is similar to getting married. We have talked about the ceremony aspect here, but it's more than just the ceremony that we're talking about. When we are baptized, we turn away from all other relationships, activities, and things that might be considered as idols, which may rival our devotion to Jesus. By repentance we turn from them and become devoted completely to Jesus.

The New Testament Greek word for "repentance" is *metanoia*, which woodenly means to have "another mind" or "a change of mind."[17] New Testament authors use various forms of this term for repentance several dozen times, including where it means something like "feel remorse or regret" or even "to be converted." Thus, repentance is associated with sorrow, even to the point of sackcloth and ashes (Luke 10:13; 2 Cor. 7:7). In 2 Corinthians 7:11, the signs that one is repentant include such things as earnestness, eagerness to clear yourself, indignation, and alarm at your current state of affairs, with a longing to see wrongs made right. Repentance is associated with remorse, but because it is connected to salvation, it is also a matter of great joy. As Jesus says, "There is joy in heaven when a sinner repents" (Luke 15:7).

It's a decision to make a change, to turn around and go a different direction. Christian repentance is what happens when our faith in Christ causes us to turn away from sin. The Bible is clear that repentance is at the heart of the Christian faith. We cannot properly embrace Jesus Christ in faith as our Lord of lords and King of kings unless we simultaneously pledge to turn from our sin and repent. God offers us healing from our sin, but by faith, we must be willing to give up sinful lifestyles and patterns.

True conversion is like a two-sided coin—one side is repentance and the other side is discipleship. One side is faith expressing itself by our turning away from sin; the other side is faith expressing itself by our commitment to trust and follow Jesus. Just as you cannot have a one-sided coin, we can't move toward a full commitment to one thing or person without simultaneously turning away from that which pulls us in the opposite direction.

The following passages give us a picture of this type of biblical repentance:

Acts 3:19: Repent, then, and turn to God, so that your sins may be wiped out, that times of refreshing may come from the Lord.

Acts 20:21: I have declared to both Jews and Greeks that they must turn to God in repentance and have faith in our Lord Jesus.

Acts 26:20: First to those in Damascus, then to those in Jerusalem and in all Judea, and to the Gentiles also, I preached that they should repent and turn to God and prove their repentance by their deeds.

Each of these passages describes repentance as an integral part of saving faith in Jesus Christ, essential for those who wish to receive his salvation and enter into life as a disciple of Jesus. God's Word connects the dynamics of faith and repentance with the act of baptism. In the following passage from Acts, Peter calls people to baptism as a concrete commitment to God, through both repentance and faith.

Acts 2:37-38: When the people heard this, they were cut to the heart and said to Peter and the other apostles, "Brothers, what shall we do?" Peter replied, "Repent and be baptized, every one of you, in the name of Jesus Christ for the forgiveness of your sins. And you will receive the gift of the Holy Spirit."

The book of Romans contains a long section describing how a believer has pledged to turn from sin to live a new life in God. Paul uses the metaphor of death: a convert pledges to die to the controlling influence of the sinful nature and place their faith in Christ. They receive life, and their death to self leads to this new life. This is all directly tied to baptism:

Romans 6:3-5: Or don't you know that all of us who were baptized into Christ Jesus were baptized into his death? We were therefore buried with him through baptism into death in order that, just as Christ was raised from the dead through the glory of the Father, we too may live a new life.

Baptism, as a reenactment of the death, burial, and resurrection of Christ, is immersion in water, symbolizing our death to sin and renewal to life. Baptism marks the beginning of a new life, marked by death to self and rising to God's life. The dying and subsequent rising becomes the pattern for the rest of our lives—we are constantly dying to selfish and sinful ways and asking God to raise us up to life in Christ (Rom. 6:17; Col. 2:12). We are baptized by immersion into water to symbolize our death and resurrection, and then we continue to live baptized lives—lives of constant dying to self and rising to Christ.

Some have claimed that these passages refer to "Spirit baptism," not water baptism. But the Bible says that there is one baptism with two parts: water and Spirit (Eph. 4:5; John 3:3-5). Water baptism and Spirit baptism normally occurred at the same time in God's Word (John 3:3-5; Acts 2:38; 1 Cor. 6:11; Tit. 3:3-6).[18]

People will often bring up Romans 6 and say that it refers to Spirit baptism only. But the perspective of the highly respected British scholar John Stott makes the most sense here. He states the following with regard to the question of whether or not it is Spirit baptism alone: "It is safe to say that whenever the terms 'baptism' and 'being baptized' occur, without mention of the element in which baptism takes place, the reference is to water baptism."[19] In alignment with Stott's comment here, Romans 6 connects water baptism to repentance.[20] The context of Romans 6 points to water baptism because it was primarily in water baptism in the Bible that one pledged to put off one's sin and live for Christ. The context here is the commitment these people made to God by their baptism, not what the Spirit of God did. Spirit baptism is what *God does*; water baptism is what *we do*.

If we hold to the ancient belief of one baptism with two parts— water and Spirit—things come together nicely. This is confirmed by the context of Romans 6, where the Roman Christians "obeyed a form of teaching" (6:17), and were later made alive by the Spirit (8:1ff). In this way, Christians naturally look back to their baptism as a turning point in their lives—the end of the old way and the beginning of God's new way, in the Spirit.

Baptism turns us from our sinful past and points to the future as disciples of Jesus. As Peter said in Acts 3:19-21:

Repent, then, and turn to God, so that your sins may be wiped out, that times of refreshing may come from the Lord, and that he may send the Messiah, who has been appointed for you—even Jesus. Heaven must receive him until the time comes for God to restore everything, as he promised long ago through his holy prophets.

CHAPTER 6

The Holy Spirit of Baptism
The Baptism of the Holy Spirit Normally Occurs in Conjunction with Water Baptism

One of life's little joys is comparing how children look to how their parents look. Especially as we grow older, we tend to take on the traits of one or both of our parents—their hair color, their eyes, their smiles, and even their way of walking. And why shouldn't we look like our parents? We are born with their genetic DNA in every single cell in our bodies.

In the same way, the Word of God says that when we are born of water, we are also born of *the Spirit* (John 3:3-5). Paul describes our reception of the Spirit as a sort of "stamp" or "seal" of the image of God (2 Cor. 1:22; Eph. 1:13-14). Water baptism marks our new birth, and the Holy Spirit becomes our genetic makeup. Upon our profession of faith in water baptism, we receive the Spirit of God, who transforms us into the image of Jesus "from one degree of glory to another" (2 Cor. 3:17-18). Being born of water and the Spirit starts a long journey in the life of the believer of conforming to the genetic DNA of God who, through the Holy Spirit, has been poured out into our hearts.

It is a big surprise to hear people answer the question, "How do you know if someone is a true Christian?" Many answers can be given, but God's Word says that the Holy Spirit is the distinguishing mark given to delineate a Christian from a non-Christian (Acts 19:1-5; Rom. 8:9; Eph. 1:13-14). We know that we are a true Christian when we see the genetic make of Jesus displayed in us through the Holy Spirit. The Spirit of God was normally given to the believer at the point of water baptism, according to Acts 2:38, Titus 3:5, and John 3:3-5. This pattern is maintained amidst some apparent ambiguity in other places in the Bible.[21]

The indwelling Spirit marks one as a Christian, and the Bible describes this reality with several similar phrases:

1) One is "baptized in the Spirit" (1 Cor. 12:13)

2) The Spirit is "poured out" (Acts 10:45)

3) We receive the "promise of the Spirit" (Acts 2:33)

4) The "gift of the Spirit" (Acts 2:38)

5) The Spirit will "come upon you" (Acts 11:15)

These are different ways of describing the coming of the Holy Spirit to dwell within and establish a person as a child of God.[22] Thus, every person who is a Christian has been "baptized in the Holy Spirit" and received "the indwelling of the Holy Spirit." As 1 Corinthians says, "For we were all baptized by one Spirit into one body—whether Jews or Greeks, slave or free—and we were all given the one Spirit to drink" (1 Cor. 12:13).[23]

In the following passages, notice the dynamic interplay between water and Spirit:

> But when the kindness and love of God our Savior appeared, he saved us, not because of righteous things we had done, but because of his mercy. He saved us through the *washing of rebirth* and *renewal by the Holy Spirit*, whom he poured out on us generously through Jesus Christ our Savior, so that having been justified by his grace, we might become heirs having the hope of eternal life. (Tit. 3:4–7)

> But *you were washed*, you were sanctified, you were justified in the name of the Lord Jesus Christ and *by the Spirit of our God*. (1 Cor. 6:11)

Jesus answered, "I tell you the truth, no one can enter the kingdom of God unless he is born of *water* and the *Spirit*." (John 3:5)[24]

As pointed out earlier, the normative description in the Bible is that baptism in water and baptism in the Spirit occur at the same time. This is true even though the Spirit sometimes follows water baptism and sometimes precedes it. But according to Acts 2:38-39, the norm is for the Spirit to be given at the point of water baptism. There are several exceptions to this in the book of Acts—exceptions that seem tied to extraordinary moments in the Christian movement, such as the conversion of the first Samaritans (Acts 8:12-17), where the Spirit comes considerably after water baptism, and the conversion of Cornelius (Acts 10:44-48), where the Spirit is poured out just prior to water baptism."[25]

This truth lies behind the biblical account of the re-baptism of twelve disciples of John in Acts 19. The Apostle Paul traveled through Ephesus, where he met men who had been followers of John the Baptist. Paul asked if they had received the Holy Spirit. When they said they had not even heard about the Holy Spirit, Paul instantly knew there was an error in their baptism:

While Apollos was at Corinth, Paul took the road through the interior and arrived at Ephesus. There he found some disciples and asked them, "Did you receive the Holy Spirit when you believed?" They answered, "No, we have not even heard that there is a Holy Spirit." So Paul asked, "Then what baptism did you receive?" "John's baptism," they replied. Paul said, "John's baptism was a baptism of repentance. He told the people to believe in the one coming after him, that is, in Jesus." On hearing this, they were baptized into the name of the Lord Jesus. When Paul placed his hands on them, the Holy Spirit came on them, and they spoke in tongues and prophesied. There were about twelve men in all. (Acts 19:1-7)

Paul's solution to an improper understanding of and relationship with the Holy Spirit was two-fold: 1) gaining a proper belief about Jesus Christ and 2) being baptized into water in the name of Jesus. In order to confirm Paul's teaching and show that God was now grafting these followers of John the Baptist into the mainstream of Christianity with their baptism, these twelve men were also enabled to speak in tongues and prophesy. This passage highlights that baptism is the typical—or "normative" as we like to call it—point in the Bible at which a person receives the indwelling Spirit.

I (Bobby) had a friend who held back from committing his life to Jesus through baptism for many years.[26] He was a highly respected medical scientist, so I assumed that his barrier to faith was intellectual. He kept saying that he was not ready. Then, one day I figured out what was holding him back; he is a very sincere person with high moral standards, and suddenly it became clear: he knew that he could never live up to the high calling that Jesus was calling him to live. He didn't want to fail, so he held back from committing.

This is a common problem, and it often surfaces as a question: "Do I have the strength and ability to be a disciple of Jesus?" We are glad people ask this question because it tells us they are taking the call to follow Jesus seriously. But our answer to this question is always the same: "No... you do not have the strength and ability. You don't have what it takes." No one has the strength, no one the ability—in their self—to follow Jesus, be changed by Jesus, and join the kingdom mission of Jesus. Without that truth, we'd be missing the good news of the gospel! Those who think this way still harbor the false hope that they can somehow try harder and do better. They haven't given in to the truth that they need a savior. We don't need a hand to help us; we need to be raised from the dead!

The gospel is good news because it tells us that none of us are good enough or strong enough to do what Jesus asks. But God promises that if we repent and surrender to Jesus, God himself through his Holy Spirit will give us the strength and ability to trust and follow Jesus. God works through our weakness, our failures, and our mistakes, and enables us to follow Jesus by the presence and power of his Holy Spirit. God, in his Holy Spirit, gives us his very DNA. And through him, from one degree of glory to another, we become like Jesus.

CHAPTER 7

The Age of Baptism
Biblical Baptism is Not for Infants

There was a young couple talking about marriage. Their relationship was moving along nicely. They had so much in common, and they shared many common dreams for a life together. But one day the young man decided to share what he disliked about his wife's family. He didn't think it would be a big deal. He and his girlfriend had made a commitment to be transparent about virtually everything, and so far, that had gone smoothly. So when he shared his thoughts about this, he couldn't believe her negative reaction.

This young man didn't realize that by criticizing what his fiancée's family had done, she would think he was criticizing her parents' character and rejecting her entire family. She was very upset, to say the least. In fact, she was so upset that she called into question the prospect of their marriage together. His criticism was a huge deal to her because family is a touchy subject for anyone.

In a similar way, as we approach the contents of this chapter, we realize that what we say may be a big challenge for you. So, let us clarify upfront what we are *not saying*:

- We are not questioning the motives and the hearts of those who practice infant baptism.

- We are not diminishing the faith of parents, nor are we attacking the genuineness of the faith of those who uphold infant baptism.

- We are not criticizing those who want to dedicate their children to God.

We value and seek to honor the faith of all who seek to trust and follow Jesus, regardless of their traditions. We think that God looks at the heart, and that is where we want to look, as well (Acts 16:9).

But we want to know what God's Word teaches us and how we can follow it. There are many different beliefs in the Christian world about when a person is ready for baptism. By following God's Word, we've found several principles to guide this topic.

First, a person must believe in Jesus Christ to be baptized. In the longer ending of Mark's Gospel, Jesus says, "*Whoever believes and is baptized* shall be saved" (Mark 16:16). Then, Peter describes baptism as the point at which a person was saved because it was at that time that they *pledged a good conscience to God* (1 Pet. 3:21; Acts 22:16). God's Word indicates that only those capable of personally believing in Jesus, pledging a good conscience, and calling on his name were baptized.

Second, as noted above, baptism is a pledge of repentance. On the day of Pentecost, Peter told at least three thousand people that they were to "repent and be baptized" (Acts 2:38). The promised gift of the Holy Spirit and the forgiveness of sins were available only to those who could repent and be baptized. Thus, to be baptized, a person should be at a point of moral development where they realize the wrongs they have committed and their need to repent of their actions to be right with God.

These are important distinctions because in the Old Testament God's people were born into the faith. Jewish parents made the decision for their children. Infants were automatically put into the community of faith when their parents had them circumcised. But the New Covenant is different: it is only open to those who will repent and follow Jesus Christ by faith.

The difference is that in the New Testament parents could not make a faith commitment for their children. Biblical faith is one in which the person enters into a saving relationship with God *only by their personal choice.*[27] Notice how the Apostle Paul contrasted the two systems of Old Testament circumcision and New Testament baptism:

In him you were also circumcised, in the putting off of the sinful nature, not with a circumcision done by the hands of men but with the circumcision done by Christ, having been buried with him in baptism and raised with him *through your faith in the power of God*, who raised him from the dead. When you were dead in your sins and in the uncircumcision of your sinful nature, God made you alive with Christ. He forgave us all our sins. (Col. 2:11-13)

"The hands of men" circumcised infants who did not have (and could not have) faith at that point in life. Their parents acted for them. That's why baptism is unlike circumcision, because in baptism the one being baptized expresses "their faith in the power of God."

Baptism in the Bible is an expression of and commitment to personal faith. In this sense, it is not something that parents can do for their children. If we are to follow the Bible, the only people eligible for baptism are those old enough to make the personal decision to turn away from their sins and trust in Jesus Christ.

This also explains the reason infant baptism did not become a common practice in church history until hundreds of years after the Bible had been fully written. The first clearly recorded infant baptism dates to the latter part of the second century (100 years after the Bible was written). We know this because the church father Tertullian opposed it on the grounds that it would be safer and more profitable to wait until faith was formed in the believing adult. Infant baptism did not become an established practice until the fourth century.[28] Even the respected professor and author Kenneth Stewart—who serves as a seminary professor for churches that support infant baptism—admits infant baptism has little objective support. In his writings, he says that he finds no clear evidence in the Bible or in the earliest years of church history that supports infant baptism.[29]

We want to summarize the reasons for what we believe. Here are six truths that direct us away from supporting infant baptism:

1. There are no passages of Scripture *that clearly teach* infant baptism in the New Testament.

2. There are no clear *examples* of infant baptism in the New Testament. All of the clear and unambiguous examples are believers who were baptized (Acts 8: 36ff; 22:16; etc.). The ones that are not clear were "households" that were baptized in the Bible (Acts 11:14), but a careful reading shows that households included their "relatives and close friends," and these are clearly adults (Acts 10:24-27). To add infants to this description is to add something that must be read into the text.

3. The New Testament correlates circumcision—as a sign that one is in the covenant—not with baptism but with the indwelling Holy Spirit (Rom. 2:29), given when a person believes in Christ (Eph. 1:13-14). This means that infant circumcision is *not* correlated to infant baptism.

4. Believer's baptism—when those who personally believe are baptized—was the practice of the church in the years immediately after the Bible was written, which excluded infants.

5. The tradition of infant baptism substitutes what the Bible clearly teaches. Almost all scholars teach that believer's baptism is biblical. Those who practice infant baptism, however, follow something that must be *read into the New Testament*. In the process, something that is (at best) an inference becomes a substitute and a replacement for the Bible's clear teaching.

6. Infant baptism does not require faith on the part of the person being baptized. Since justification can only be granted through faith, infant baptism skews the teaching of God's Word about faith.

In summary, if we are seeking to follow God's Word, the following three guidelines will help us apply the biblical truths we've covered in this section. First, only those who believe can be baptized. Second, repentance from sin, coupled with the commitment to live as a disciple of Jesus, must be a driving factor in baptism. Third, there is no clear support in the Bible or in the earliest years of the church to support infant baptism.

CHAPTER 8

The Method of Baptism

Biblical Baptism is Performed by Immersion

A second century B.C. physician, Nicander of Colophon, was an early health-food champion. One of the Nicander's recipes describes how to make pickled radishes—and his recipe helps us understand how to baptize in the twenty-first century.

How can pickled radishes help us understand baptism? Nicander uses two terms that are also used in the New Testament. First, he says, you should dip *(bapto)* the radishes in boiling water. Then, Nicander says, you should soak *(baptizo)* the radishes in vinegar. Of course we are not interested in radishes in this book, but we are interested in the terms that are translated "baptism" in the New Testament.

As Nicander and many other Greek authors from the biblical era reveal, the terms most frequently translated "baptism" inherently involve the act of dipping and soaking… even sloshing around. To pickle radishes, you dip them, then soak them. In the same way, to baptize a person into Christ, you dip them in water, and soak them in the Spirit.

The same Greek word is used in the New Testament for baptism: *baptizo*. It means "to dip, plunge, or to immerse."[30] If God had wanted us to follow a different method of baptizing, then it would have been reflected by the use of other words to describe it. If he had meant to say "pour," for instance, he might have used *ekcheo*, which is Greek for "to pour out." If he wanted to say "sprinkle," he could have used *rantizo*, which means, "to sprinkle." God intends baptism to be by immersion because without exception, every writer in the New Testament used the Greek word *baptizein* when describing the act.[31] We know that when the writers of the New Testament speak of baptism, they mean immersion because that is what *baptizein* means.[32]

Even if, for the sake of argument, the word for baptism in the original text was not baptizien, we can still determine the nature of baptism by context clues in the New Testament. One of the clearest examples comes from Romans 6, which we addressed above. The Apostle Paul wanted to remind the early Christians of the need to live holy lives. In order to remind them of God's grace and their original commitment, Paul recalled the time when they were baptized, describing baptism as a drama with three distinct acts. The first act is death: when a person goes into the water, they pledge to identify themselves with Christ's death (v. 3). The second act is a burial: in this burial in water, a person reenacts the burial of Christ (v. 4). The third act is a resurrection: in coming out of the water, a person is raised to live a new kind of life (vv. 4-5). Whenever a person was baptized in the New Testament, there was a reenactment of the death, burial, and resurrection of Jesus. No action except immersion communicates this rich biblical principle.

> Or don't you know that all of us who were baptized into Christ Jesus were baptized into his death? We were therefore buried with him through baptism into death in order that, just as Christ was raised from the dead through the glory of the Father, we too may live a new life. If we have been united with him like this in his death, we will certainly also be united with him in his resurrection. (Rom. 6:3-5)

As such, even without the Greek language background, one can see the practice of baptism must be by immersion because it enacts with Christ our death, burial, and resurrection to new life.

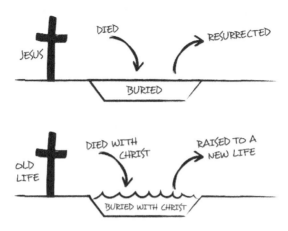

That is, the form goes with the function. Immersion puts us into Christ's death and raises us to new life. This makes the form itself an important beginning to our life of discipleship. Baptism is the death and resurrection of one's self, serving as a pattern for the rest of our lives—we are constantly dying to self and rising with Christ (Rom. 6:17). Paul makes the same point in Colossians 2:11-12.[33]

We believe it's unwise to look at immersion as simply a cultural practice used to express faith in Christ in the first century. These passages show that the meaning of the commitment to follow Christ *cannot be separated* from the method used to make the commitment—the meaning is tied to the method. Full immersion in water is a concrete expression of Christian conversion. In this practice a person enters the death, burial, and resurrection of Jesus. Thus, only immersion symbolizes that which lies at the heart of conversion and the entire Christian life—death to self and identification with Christ.

CHAPTER 9

The Obligation of Baptism
While We Recognize God Saves Whom He Wills, We are Bound to Stand on Biblical Baptism

Sometimes families have to sit down for a serious talk. That's what this chapter feels like. At a family talk we ask everyone to prioritize the meeting and cancel other appointments. We ask everyone to turn off their devices and fully engage in the conversation. We set it up this way because sometimes we have to talk about hard things. This topic seems difficult to talk about on a personal level because various nuances are difficult or it's just difficult to address. In this chapter, we need to talk about something that is hard and nuanced.

First, the hard part of this chapter.

We pointed out that instead of asking people to respond to Jesus' finished work on the cross by expressing faith and repentance in baptism, many evangelical churches encourage people to receive Jesus as Lord and Savior by saying a prayer. Through this prayer, people invite Jesus to "come into their hearts." As we mentioned, this approach to becoming a Christian is not found in the Bible, in the creeds, or in early church history.[34]

Most don't know this, but the sinner's prayer has only been utilized for the last one hundred years. Paul Chitwood researched this background and presented it as his Ph.D. dissertation at Southern Baptist Theological Seminary.[35] He demonstrates that it was popularized by Campus Crusade's Bill Bright (through "The Four Spiritual Laws") and Billy Graham, likely starting in the 1930s or 1940s.

Renew leaders agree that many people and churches have missed the biblical emphasis on a relationship with God through trusting

Jesus in our hearts. We believe that many do not hear enough that we are saved by grace through faith. And we know one Scripture passage that seems to point to something similar to the sinner's prayer: Romans 10:10, which says, "For it is with your heart that you believe and are justified, and it is with your mouth that you confess and are saved." A confession like this is a good thing, in and of itself, even if it is done apart from baptism, as the Bible teaches. But it is not a substitute for baptism.

Thus, the sinner's prayer is not the full biblical response.[36] Many Bible-believing churches have rejected the role of baptism in personal conversion in a reaction to a legalistic view of baptism by Roman Catholic, Orthodox, and other churches. In so doing, however, they have gone too far and rejected what we see as the biblical path. While nothing like the sinner's prayer exists in the book of Acts, Acts is replete with references to baptism at the very places we might expect to find the sinner's prayer.[37] The book of Acts clearly shows that baptism, not the sinner's prayer, was the method given by God to express and place one's faith in Jesus Christ.

Baptism in the Bible was not something done after conversion. Baptism is how we express our faith for the forgiveness of sins and how we experience conversion. When the sinner's prayer becomes the method of receiving the forgiveness of sins, it replaces baptism as the method. Then a new meaning has to be attached to baptism. So in addition to not finding the sinner's prayer in the Word of God, we cannot find any verses that explicitly state the following alleged purposes of baptism:

- Baptism is the first step of obedience
- Baptism is a public demonstration of our faith
- Baptism is an outward sign of an inward reality
- Baptism is a sign or seal of salvation already received

None of these statements are from the Bible, and all of them assume salvation before baptism.

Instead of these expressions, when investigating the Word of God, you will find that men and women hear the gospel, believe it, and are baptized to express their faith and find forgiveness and a saving relationship with God:

- Acts 2:37-38, 41: When they heard this... Peter said, "Repent and be baptized, every one of you, in the name of Jesus Christ for the forgiveness of your sins..." Those who welcomed his message were baptized.

- Acts 8:11-12: They listened eagerly to him...when they believed... they were baptized, both men and women.

- Acts 8:13: Simon himself believed. After being baptized, he stayed constantly with Philip.

- Acts 8:35-36: Philip... told him the good news about Jesus... they came to some water and the eunuch said, "Look here is water. Why shouldn't I be baptized?"

- Acts 16:14-15: Lydia, a worshiper of God, was listening to us... The Lord opened her heart to listen eagerly...When she and her household were baptized...

- Acts 16:31-33: Believe in the Lord Jesus, and you will be saved—you and your household... then he and his entire family were baptized without delay.

- Acts 18:8: Many of the Corinthians who heard him believed and were baptized.

- Acts 19:5: On hearing this, they were baptized in the name of the Lord Jesus.

These texts call attention to the language and frequency with which baptism immediately follows receiving the word or believing the gospel. You do not find anything like the sinner's prayer in these conversions.

The following chart highlights the same truths:

TEXT	HEARD	BELIEVED	REPENTED	BAPTIZED	HOLY SPIRIT	SAVED
Pentecost Acts 2:14-41	Heard 2:37	Believed 2:37	Repented 2:38	Baptized 2:41	At Immersion 2:38	Remission of Sins 2:38
Samaria Acts 8:5-13	Heard 8:12	Believed 8:13		Baptized 8:12-13	After Immersion 8:15-17	
Eunuch Acts 8:35-39	Heard 8:35	Believed 8:36		Baptized 8:38-39		Rejoicing 8:39
Saul Acts 9:1-18; 22:1-16; 26:9-18	Heard 9:4-6	Believed 22:10	Repented 9:9	Baptized 9:18	At Immersion 9:17-18	Washed Away Sins 22:16
Cornelius Acts 10:34-48 11:4-18; 15:7-11	Heard 10:44; 11:14	Believed 10:43	Repented 11:18	Baptized 10:48	Before Immersion 10:46-47	Purified Hearts 15:9
Lydia Acts 16:13-15	Heard 16:14	Believed 16:14		Baptized 16:15		
Jailor Acts 16:30-34	Heard 16:32	Believed 16:31	Repented 16:33	Baptized 16:33		Rejoiced 16:34
Corinthians Acts 18:8	Heard 18:8	Believed 18:8		Baptized 18:8		
Ephesians Disciples Acts 19:1-7	Heard 19:2	Believed 19:2		Baptized 19:5	After Immersion 19:6	

The book of Acts clearly shows that baptism, not the sinner's prayer, was the method given by God to place one's faith in Jesus Christ.

In the New Testament, people were baptized without delay. People were commanded to do this on the day of Pentecost, after hearing about Christ's salvation for the first time, even from a large crowd (Acts 2:38-42). They also did it in the midst of a long trip, immediately after hearing about salvation through Jesus (Acts 8: 36-40). And a jailer temporarily took his prisoners, Paul and Silas, out of the jail in the middle of the night, so he and his family could immediately be baptized (Acts 16:31-33). This immediate practice of baptism, contrary to what many churches do today, shows us what the first Christians really believed. People would not have felt this urgency for baptism unless it was God's normative way to express saving faith to become a Christian.

This was also the viewpoint of the early church in the period immediately following the writing of the New Testament. Consider the words of the earliest Church Fathers (the first leaders after the New Testament):

> Blessed are those who placed their hope in his cross and descended into water… we descend into the water full of sins and uncleanliness, and we ascend bearing reverence in our heart and having hope in Jesus in our spirit. (*Epistle of Barnabas*, 11.1, 8, 11)

> Then they are led by us to where there is water, and in the manner of the new birth by which we ourselves were born again they are born again. For at that time they obtain for themselves the washing in water in the name of God the Master of all and Father, and of our Savior Jesus Christ and of the Holy Spirit. For Christ said, "Unless you are born again, you cannot enter the kingdom of heaven." (Justin Martyr, *Apology*, 1.6)

> Now this is what faith does for us, as the elders, the disciples of the apostles, have handed down to us. First of all, it admonishes us to remember that we have received baptism for the remission of sins in the name of God the Father, and in the name of Jesus Christ, the Son of God, who became incarnate and died and was raised, and in the Holy Spirit of God; and that this baptism is the seal of eternal life and is rebirth into God. (Irenaeus, *Proof of the Apostolic Preaching*, 3)

Again, as the respected scholar of the ancient church Everett Ferguson points out in his book *Baptism in the Early Church*, these statements typify the early Christian consensus.[38] Early Christians viewed baptism as the instrumental means given by God to place one's faith in Christ, receive his forgiveness, and commit oneself to the path of discipleship. Renew leaders, therefore, stand with both biblical teaching and the early church in this position on baptism.

Now, for the more nuanced part of this chapter.

Our position does not necessitate the belief that God can only save those who experience biblical baptism. While we are committed to the same practice as the New Testament and the early church, we believe it is another thing to say a follower of Christ cannot be saved unless they have been properly baptized. We cannot make such a statement because God is always the one who grants salvation.[39] He is the judge, not us—and he looks at his ordinances and human hearts in ways we cannot see.

God alone is sovereign; he saved people in Jesus' day who had faith but did not experience John's baptism, which was for the forgiveness of sins (Matt. 9:2-5; Luke 3:3; 7:46-48; 23:40-43). God is free to do the same today, but we are not at liberty to do this. Indeed, most Renew leaders have adopted the position articulated by Robert Fife many years ago when he said, "We ought never forget that he [God] is the Lord whose freedom as well as faithfulness to the covenant people must respect. There is wisdom in the ancient aphorism, *God is not bound to the sacraments, though man is.*"[40] God can save anyone he chooses, but *we are bound* to teach and practice biblical baptism.

Further, the Bible and history show that God's acceptance of human faith is not always predicated on strict adherence to proper ritual.[41] Personal and deeply rooted faith in Jesus is far more important than an external form given as the means to express this faith—though both are important.[42] We want to practice carefully what God has instituted with regard to baptism while still testifying that a transformed, Christ-centered life gives evidence to the presence of the Holy Spirit as *the true mark* that shows God has saved someone.[43]

And while we cannot be certain that God has truly given his Holy Spirit to someone else (only God knows that),[44] we show wisdom when we acknowledge that God's saving power is at work in many Christ followers who have not experienced biblical baptism.[45] So we are bound to practice what Scripture sets out.

In summary, we state this: ***Baptism, as an expression of faith, is for the remission of sins, and baptism is the normative means of entry into the life of discipleship.*** Thus, we uphold the normative biblical model, but we acknowledge that God looks at the heart and can mysteriously work in the lives of those who trust him, however he sees fit.

As a wedding ceremony should make a marriage formal and complete, so water baptism should formalize and complete our new relationships with God. In the Bible, this was the special time in which the miracle of salvation typically occurred. In this sense, as stated above, we must reclaim the teaching that baptism—as an expression of faith in Jesus—is "for the remission of sins" (Acts 2:38).

CHAPTER 10

The Commitment of Baptism
Biblical Baptism is a Commitment to Become a Disciple of Jesus

I (David) once knew a man who had struggled with an addiction for years before coming to faith in Jesus. I thought that if only he were baptized, that would stop his temptations, but it didn't. Indeed, he remarked, "I started craving my sinful addiction within hours after my baptism." Though he did not return to his sin, he couldn't stop feeling that there was something wrong with him because he still craved certain temptations. Was there something so filthy inside him that even Jesus couldn't heal him?

After months of struggle, he came to realize that, though justification is a one-time event, sanctification (growth in Christlikeness) is a life-long process. He began to think of his baptism not as failed medicine, but as a guarantee that Christ was with him. Years later, he explained to me how his baptism eventually played a role in overcoming his temptation. His words are worth including here: "Every time the Devil would whisper in my ear that I was not good enough to follow Jesus, I would point back to my baptism and remind the Devil that Jesus had married me. I wear the wedding ring of the King of kings. If Jesus is willing to call me his spouse, then who are you to question me?"

Because baptism is a form of commitment, it brings with it a deep sense of security. Before Jesus left the earth, he gave the Great Commission to his disciples. Those of us who are disciples today also receive this teaching as a mandate to make disciples:

> Then, Jesus came to them and said, "All authority in heaven and on earth has been given to me. Therefore go and make

disciples of all nations, baptizing them in the name of the Father and of the Son and of the Holy Spirit, and teaching them to obey everything I have commanded you. And surely I am with you always, to the very end of the age." (Matthew 28:18-20)

In the Greek text of Matthew 28:19, there is a primary imperative command in this verse, which we translate "make disciples."[46] This command is modified by three phrases describing *how we are to make disciples*. We make disciples in three ways: by 1) going, 2) baptizing, and 3) teaching obedience to all of Jesus' commands. Additionally, we are always trusting and relying on the presence of the Holy Spirit.

Let's look more closely at baptism in this passage. We are to make disciples of all nations by "baptizing them in the name of the Father and of the Son and of the Holy Spirit." Baptizing "into the name of" means we are baptizing people by the authority of the triune God and into a relationship with him as Father, Son, and Holy Spirit.[47]

There's more: baptism is the inauguration into a life of being a disciple. We have been baptized in the authority of the triune God so that we can now obey all the commands of Christ. And we know that he is with us—"to the very end of the age." Various places in the New Testament state that baptism is a commitment to discipleship. As repentance is a key part of discipleship—we turn from following sinful lifestyles to following Christ—so is repentance a key part of baptism (Acts 2:38; 1 Pet. 3:21). Likewise, both Colossians 2:12-3:5 and Romans 6:1-17 explicitly connect baptism to our commitment to live a new life. Romans 6:4-5 in particular states it this way:

We were therefore buried with him through baptism into death in order that, just as Christ was raised from the dead through the glory of the Father, we too may live a new life. If we have been united with him like this in his death, we will certainly also be united with him in his resurrection.

We are baptized so that we may live a *new life*. Paul goes on to state the reality of what our baptism commits us to in Romans 6:11-13:

> In the same way, count yourselves dead to sin but alive to God in Christ Jesus. Therefore, do not let sin reign in your mortal body so that you obey its evil desires. Do not offer any part of yourself to sin as an instrument of wickedness, but rather offer yourselves to God as those who have been brought from death to life; and offer every part of yourself to him as an instrument of righteousness.

This is the life of a disciple of Jesus. This passage describes our goal. As Paul says, after our baptism he commands us to offer ourselves to God as those who have been brought from death to life, and offer every part of ourselves to him as an instrument of righteousness. Romans makes it clear that we are committing ourselves to this path of discipleship by our baptism, but remember that discipleship is a process. We must learn how to offer our bodies as instruments of righteousness. We need the help of others, as well as the direction of the Word of God and the Spirit of God.

As the leader of a worldwide seminary with hundreds of students enrolled annually, I (Tony) have the privilege of serving many former Muslims. I always like to ask them why they made a radical commitment to Christ, having come from an Islamic background. Once they've been baptized, some lose jobs, friends, families, or status, or receive death threats—or a combination of those. One barely prevented the gang rape of his wife and two young daughters when he became a believer. Their answers share so many commonalities.

They are now free from sin, guilt, shame, fear, and jihad. They have come to someone who not only saved them but also set them free to serve his higher mission. They have new callings, friends, family, purpose, and status. Now, they have a Father who loves them so much that he includes them into his family and work. They truly believe their commitment to the Father gives them a life infinitely more valuable than any sacrifice they've made. That's the commitment of baptism.

CHAPTER 11

The Timing of Baptism
Baptism Marks One's Entrance into the Church

Throughout Christian history and still in certain locations to-day, churches have been known to rename people once they've been baptized. One North American church we know of renamed a young man "Zeal" upon his baptism; a Ghanaian church once renamed a person "Patience" upon her baptism; a Greek church started calling one of its members "Charis" (meaning "grace") upon her baptism. The early church started to call one of their leaders, a man formerly named Joseph, "the encourager" ("Barnabas"). Indeed, the history of naming in Western Europe includes both common names and so-called Christian names.

Name changes can signal several things, but for many churches it signals that baptism has brought one into a new family—the local family of God. It is a beautiful thing that one's baptism in water signifies new birth into a new community. As the Apostle Paul says, "For we were all baptized by one Spirit into one body—whether Jews or Greeks, slave or free—and we were all given the one Spirit to drink" (1 Cor. 12:13). In baptism, we celebrate our new life in the local church.

We believe that the experience of biblical baptism should occur prior to membership or a formal commitment to a local church. This approach to church means that we help inquirers commit themselves to Christ in baptism before they become a part of the church as a covenant community. It also means that we often baptize those who have faith in Christ and years of commitment to him but have not experienced a biblical baptism.

Many come to our churches who have an intimate and spiritual relationship with Jesus but were never taught what the Bible says about baptism. Some simply don't know about the rich blessing offered to us in biblical baptism. For these people, our churches typically offer more teaching and, without judging their past or their other churches, the opportunity to deepen their obedience to Scripture by being baptized.

I (David) once preached in a church that had never really considered what the Bible says about baptism. When I pointed out to them what the Scriptures teach, many were baptized, and their lead pastor began teaching the beauty of baptism. This is like what happened with Priscilla and Aquila. We help people who have been walking with Jesus for many years before learning of the proper teaching on baptism:

> Meanwhile a Jew named Apollos, a native of Alexandria, came to Ephesus. He was a learned man, with a thorough knowledge of the Scriptures. He had been instructed in the way of the Lord, and he spoke with great fervor and taught about Jesus accurately, though he knew only the baptism of John. He began to speak boldly in the synagogue. When Priscilla and Aquila heard him, they invited him to their home and explained to him the way of God more adequately. (Acts 18:24-26)

If a follower of Jesus who has not experienced biblical baptism comes to one of our churches, we seek to explain to them the *normative, biblical way* of entering the faith. At the same time, we affirm their previous walk with Christ. But like Priscilla and Aquila with Apollos, we encourage them to experience a biblical baptism.[48] Most Christian groups in history apply this timing of baptism to their practices—before formal affiliation or recognition as a member of the covenant community—even though denominations may understand the mode of baptism differently.[49]

A related question often arises: What is a valid baptism? What does a person need to know and believe when they are being baptized in order for their baptism "to be valid"? A quick answer is that a person cannot know everything that can be known about baptism and everything that God does for us in baptism. But a person should know the basics of the gospel and what it means to have faith. They must understand what it means to repent and to turn to Jesus. We believe biblical baptism includes *repentance and trust in Jesus and commitment to follow his example by being immersed.* We sum it up this way: A person must be committed to trusting and following Jesus, and their baptism must fundamentally express that belief, even if they are not fully conscious of all the implications, including that it is for the remission of sins. Most fundamentally, we believe that baptism must express faith in Jesus and be an expression of allegiance to him. The relationship is the fundamental issue, and baptism most fundamentally must be about expressing allegiance to that relationship.

Last, we also believe that unity on this matter is very important for the sake of the spiritual seekers in our midst. The Scriptures emphasize baptism as part of the believer's new birth. If we de-emphasize or compromise this practice, we will teach people that they can disagree with plain, biblical statements. We want to be fully obedient to God's revealed will in Scripture, and we believe that when we stand firm on biblical baptism before membership, it helps everyone take this teaching seriously.

Virtually every culture and religion has various initiation rites designed to mark such things as the passage from childhood to adulthood (or one's full entrance into the community). Jews celebrate *Bar and Bat Mitzvah.* Native Americans have rituals such as "vision quests." Fraternities and sororities, although a different sort of "ceremony," have initiation rites. Various professions include certification and licensing processes that function as initiation rites, too. Even companies and businesses have welcome lunches and dinners for new employees. Such rites are important because they offer a formal mark that says a person is now a member of the community, the guild, or the organization.

In a similar way, baptism serves to indicate that a person is now "born again" into what Paul calls "the household of God" (1 Tim. 3:15). We don't want to emphasize baptism to the point that we overshadow God's grace or our faith, but baptism does offer local congregations a sort of initiation rite that indicates a person is now part of the community. Every person properly baptized is born again, and the local church provides the household where that person can celebrate their new life in community.

CONCLUSION

We believe that the view and practice of biblical baptism should be grounded in grace and faith, while affirming a holistic commitment of faith expressed by repentance and confession. We believe that the normative biblical model of conversion described in this book is the one God wants us to renew for the church of our day.

Water baptism concretely seals our repentance and commitment to Jesus Christ. Water baptism is the God-given vehicle by which we give up our sinful ways and accept Christ for salvation. Faith is the essential human response to God's saving grace, and baptism is the ceremonial means given by God for expressing it.

Our position can be summarized in the following points:

- The baptism ceremony—like the wedding ceremony—is the biblical method of commitment by which a personal covenant relationship with God is to be made.

- Baptism by immersion is integral to the conversion process and, when it expresses faith in Jesus, is for the remission of sins.

- The "sinner's prayer" and "asking Jesus into one's heart" are recent human inventions and good faith efforts to win people to Christ, but baptism is the biblical and ancient means of grace given to accept Christ by faith.

- We believe that we are bound by Scripture to uphold baptism as an expression of faith for the remission of sins, while acknowledging God's sovereign freedom to grant the Holy Spirit and forgiveness as he wills.

- The practice of biblical baptism should lead to more holistic and deeply rooted conversions because, when upheld properly, it involves clear expressions of faith, repentance, and commitment to the path of discipleship. It teaches people to obey God's Word, and it symbolizes the new life God gives us in Christ.

APPENDIX

How a Baptism Ceremony Works

There are practical questions people ask when they are considering baptism. At the forefront are questions like, "What do I need to know to be baptized?" and "What are the mechanics of the baptism ceremony itself?"

Answering questions about how much a person needs to know about Jesus, the gospel, and faith is relatively simple. After all, the Ethiopian Eunuch was baptized after hearing the gospel while on a journey in a chariot (Acts 8:26ff), and the Philippian jailer and his family were baptized in the middle of the night (Acts 16:33). These passages, among others, show us that extensive knowledge is not necessary.

There are three things people should know before a baptism:

- First, the person being baptized should understand the basics of who Jesus is, his gospel of grace, and what God promises to all of those who place their faith in him. In this knowledge, a person will be grounded in the love of God expressed for us in Christ Jesus.

- Second, the person being baptized should understand the double-sided nature of faith as an ongoing commitment. Specifically, on the one side, they need to understand what it means to repent and turn from sinful lifestyles.

- Third, they need to understand what it means to make the commitment to place their faith in Jesus, which means they will seek to trust and follow Jesus for all of life—to be an authentic disciple.

This means that candidates for baptism should have a good understanding of what the Bible teaches about sinful lifestyles and what it means to turn from them in repentance. A friend of ours says that it should at least take us as long to prepare for baptism as it does to get our driver's license. We agree.

People need clarity on the things God calls sin and the ways in which God empowers us to turn away from sinful lifestyles. Furthermore, they must be ready to fully and consciously turn from any sinful ways of living in the power that God provides and with the help of people in the church.

On the positive side, candidates for baptism must appreciate the greatness of Christ and what it means to truly follow him. They should be able to state, in explicit terms, what it means to follow Jesus and the ways in which they plan to live out this commitment and be a disciple of Jesus. They must also understand the importance of being personally discipled by others in the church, especially in the early period of the Christian life, so they become grounded in the faith. They need to understand that church involvement is essential for the life of faith (Heb. 3:10-14; 10:23-25). Once these understandings are established, a person is ready to be baptized.

While denominations practice baptism by immersion in various ways (and there's freedom within baptism by immersion), we recommend the following elements for the physical act of baptism:

Before the baptism:

1. The water is to be sufficient for full immersion. It should also be warm enough and safe. (River baptisms require advanced planning.)

2. Ensure that proper clothing for the baptism is present for both modesty and comfort. People are typically most comfortable bringing their own clothes and towels. (Churches often have garments for those who make the decision to be baptized at an unplanned time.)

3. Have the candidate for baptism change into the clothes they will wear in the baptism before starting the baptism ceremony. Make sure the person has towels.

4. It is often helpful to ask the person to write out a clear statement (typically just one page) on why they want to be baptized. This statement will often be read out loud just before the baptism. As the years go by, it will be helpful for the person to look back at what they believed when they were baptized. This is often a reassuring experience later in life.

During the baptism:

1. The one leading the baptism process will explain what the person being baptized is doing and what it will mean in their life (for the sake of the church, family, and guests).

2. If there's time, the leader may ask the person who is about to be baptized (typically while they are in the water) to explain why they are being baptized and what this commitment personally means to them. This is when they read the written statement out loud.

3. When baptizing someone in front of others, we recommend that you ask questions like these:

   a. Do you personally place trust in and rely on Jesus' work on the cross to give you the forgiveness of your sins?

   b. Do you commit to follow Jesus Christ by faith, according to the teachings of the Bible and with God as your helper for the rest of your life?

   c. Do you believe that Jesus Christ is the Son of God? And can you confess with your mouth the great confession? Then, they say, "Jesus is Lord."

4. The baptizer will have the person hold their nose with their hand (gently pinch with thumb and forefinger), as the baptizer holds with one of their hands the wrist of the one being baptized and the back of their neck with the other. The baptizer may tell the person, "As you go under the water, you express your faith in Christ to God." The baptizer may invite others to join them as they immerse the new believer in water. The Bible does not give us any requirements for the person doing the baptism, so we believe it's something any disciple of Jesus can do for another person.

5. Just before the baptizer puts the person being baptized under the water, they may state so everyone can hear, "Based upon your confession of faith, I now baptize you in the name of the Father, Son, and Holy Spirit." The baptizer will completely immerse the person in the water. They may say, as they are baptizing the person, "Buried with Christ in baptism, raised to walk in newness of life."

After the baptism:

1. Once the person being baptized comes up out of the water, spiritual leaders will often place hands on the person and pray. The prayer is simply that the Holy Spirit will richly indwell the person and that God will guide them to do good and important things as a disciple of Jesus.

2. Celebrate this decision! Sometimes afterwards parents, family, or other friends make it a big deal by having a special gathering for presents, speeches, and a meal. You may want to take pictures and record a video of the whole event.

Most importantly, there is rejoicing in the presence of the angels of God (Luke 15:10).

ENDNOTES

[1] Everett Ferguson: *Baptism in the Early Church: History, Theology, and Liturgy in the First Five Centuries* (Grand Rapids, Michigan: Wm. B. Eerdmans Publishing Co., 2009).

[2] The technical and scholarly support to this presentation is found in the highly respected work of Everett Ferguson: *Baptism in the Early Church: History, Theology, and Liturgy in the First Five Centuries* (Grand Rapids, Michigan: Wm. B. Eerdmans Publishing Co., 2009); and also, in the older work of G.R. Beasley Murry, *Baptism in the New Testament* (Grand Rapids, Michigan: Wm. B. Eerdmans Publishing Co., 1962). For information on the historical backgrounds of this view see David Fletcher, editor., *Baptism and the Remission of Sins: An Historical Perspective* (Joplin, Missouri: College Press, 1990). See also Jack P. Lewis, "Baptismal Practices of the Second and Third Century Church," *Restoration Quarterly* Vol. 26 (1983): 1-17; and Everett Ferguson, *The Early Christians* Speak (Abilene, Texas: ACU Press, reprint 1994). Our understanding is reflected in the *Nicaeno-Constantinoplotan Creed* of A.D. 381, which states, "I acknowledge one baptism for the remission of sins." See also *The Creeds of Christendom*, 3 Volumes, edited by Philip Schaff (Grand Rapids, Michigan: Baker Book House, 1996).

[3] We are grateful for the extensive work on the New Testament teaching on the gospel in Matthew Bates's forthcoming book, which we have been able to preview, *Gospel Allegiance* (Ada, MI: Brazos, 2019).

[4] Sheryl Harris, "Find out if you've got an unclaimed inheritance: Plain dealing," https://www.cleveland.com/consumeraffairs/index.ssf/2014/04/unclaimed_inheritance_database.html, accessed September 16, 2018.

[5] Many of us believe the *Armenian Creed* of A.D. 1610 is correct when it describes God's work within us, creating faith as grace. Article 3 says, "That man has not saving grace of himself, nor of the energy of his free will, inasmuch as he, in the state of apostasy and sin, can of and by himself neither think, will, nor do any thing that is truly good (such as saving faith eminently is); but that it is needful that he be born again of God in Christ, through his Holy Spirit, and renewed in understanding, inclination, or will, and all his powers, in order that he may rightly understand, think, will, and effect what is truly good, according to the Word of Christ, John 15:5: 'Without me you can do nothing.'" Article 4 states, "That this grace of God is the beginning, continuance, and accomplishment of all good, even to this extent, that the regenerate man himself, without prevenient or assisting, awakening, following and co-operative grace, can neither think, will, nor do good, nor withstand any temptations to evil; so that all good deeds or movements, that can be conceived, must be ascribed to the grace of God in Christ. But as respects the mode of the operation of this grace, it is not irresistible, inasmuch as it is written concerning many, that they have

resisted the Holy Spirit, Acts 7 and elsewhere in many places." See *The Creeds of Christendom*, 3 Volumes, edited by Philip Schaff (Grand Rapids, Michigan: Baker Book House, 1996).

[6] See Matthew Bates, *Salvation by Allegiance Alone: Rethinking Faith, Works, and the Gospel of Jesus the King* (Ida, Michigan: Baker Academic, 2017), *passim*.

[7] See respected commentator C.B. Cranfied's *Romans: A Shorter Commentary* (Grand Rapids, Michigan: Wm. B. Eerdmans Publishing, 1985), 257, where he discusses this point. With regard to *Romans* 10:9-10, he states, "It seems clear that 'Jesus is Lord' was already an established confession formula. It is probable that it was used in connection with baptism...." And even the popular NIV Study Bible points this out in its study notes on Romans 10:9. See also John Stott and Thomas Schreiner's comments on this passage which emphasize the Old Testament roots: Stott, *Romans* (Downers Grove, Illinois: InterVarsity Press, 1994), Shreiner, *Romans* (Grand Rapids, Michigan: Baker Books, 1998).

[8] Walter Kaiser, Peter Davids, F.F. Bruce, and Manfred Brauch, *Hard Sayings of the Bible* (Downers Grove, Illinois: InterVarsity Press, 1996).

[9] Some dispute the English rendition of this passage, arguing that the preposition eis ("for the") somehow means that people are baptized "because of the" forgiveness of sins (making baptism simply a symbol of salvation previously received). Technically and linguistically, this is not correct. The English translations have it right—see Jack Cottrell, *Baptism: A Biblical Study* (Joplin, Missouri: College Press, 1989), 55-61. For the syntactical and grammatical background see Carroll D. Osburn, "The Third Person Imperative in Acts 2: 38," *Restoration Quarterly* (1983): 81-84.

[10] The technical and scholarly support to this presentation is found in the highly respected work of Everett Ferguson, *Baptism in the Early Church: History, Theology, and Liturgy in the First Five Centuries* (Grand Rapids, Michigan: Wm. B. Eerdmans Publishing Co., 2009); and also, in the older work of G.R. Beasley Murry, *Baptism in the New Testament* (Grand Rapids, Michigan: Wm. B. Eerdmans Publishing Co., 1962). For information on the historical backgrounds of this view, see David Fletcher, editor, *Baptism and the Remission of Sins: An Historical Perspective* (Joplin, Missouri: College Press, 1990). See also Jack P. Lewis, "Baptismal Practices of the Second and Third Century" Church," *Restoration Quarterly* vol. 26 (1983): 1-17; and Everett Ferguson, The Early Christians Speak (Abilene, Texas: (ACU Press, reprint 1994). Our understanding is reflected in the *Nicaeno-Constantinoplotan Creed* of A.D. 381, which states, "I acknowledge one baptism for the remission of sins." See *The Creeds of Christendom*, 3 Volumes, edited by Philip Schaff (Baker Book House: Grand Rapids, Michigan, 1996).

[11] See Bill Hull, *Conversion and Discipleship: You Can't Have One Without the Other* (Grand Rapids, Michigan: Zondervan, 2016), and Bill

Hull and Ben Sobels, *The Discipleship Gospel* (Nashville, Tennessee: HIM Publications, 2018).

[12] J.D. Greear, *Stop Asking Jesus into Your Heart: How to Know For Sure You Are Saved* (Nashville, Tennessee: B & H Books, 2013).

[13] Again, the technical and scholarly support to this presentation is found in the highly respected work of Everett Ferguson: *Baptism in the Early Church: History, Theology, and Liturgy in the First Five Centuries* (Grand Rapids, Michigan: Wm. B. Eerdmans Publishing Co., 2009); and also, in the older work of G.R. Beasley Murry, *Baptism in the New Testament* (Grand Rapids, Michigan: Wm. B. Eerdmans Publishing Co., 1962). For information on the historical backgrounds of this view, see David Fletcher, editor., *Baptism and the Remission of Sins: An Historical Perspective* (Joplin, Missouri: College Press, 1990). See also Jack P. Lewis, "Baptismal Practices of the Second and Third Century Church," *Restoration Quarterly* Vol. 26 (1983): 1-17; and Everett Ferguson, *The Early Christians Speak* (Abilene, Texas: ACU Press, reprint 1994). Our understanding is reflected in the *Nicaeno-Constantinoplotan Creed* of A.D. 381, which states, "I acknowledge one baptism for the remission of sins." See *The Creeds of Christendom*, 3 Volumes, edited by Philip Schaff (Baker Book House: Grand Rapids, Michigan, 1996).

[14] For more information on the Roman Catholic position, see https://www.catholic.com/qa/what-does-the-expression-ex-opere-operato-mean, accessed September 17, 2018

[15] I. Howard Marshall, The *Acts of the Apostles*, in The Tyndale New Testament Commentaries (Grand Rapids, Michigan: InterVarsity Press, 1980), 81.

[16] For more technical work on the following approach, see H. Bietenhard, "Prepositions with baptizo," in *The International Dictionary of New Testament Theology*, edited by Colin Brown (Grand Rapids, Michigan: Zondervan Publishing Company, 1975), vol. 3: 1207-1211; Lars Hartman, "Into the Name of Jesus, " *New Testament Studies* 20 (1973): 432-440; and Lars Hartman, "Baptism Into the Name of Jesus' and Early Christianity," Studia Theologica 28 (1974): 21-48

[17] Bauer, Danker, Arndt & Gingrich, *Greek-English Lexicon of the New Testament and Other Early Christian Literature BDAG (University of Chicago Press*, 2001), 511-12.

[18] Jack Cottrell, Baptism a Biblical Study (Joplin Missouri: College Press, 1990).

[19] See this quote in John Stott, Romans: God's Good News For The World (Downers Grove, Illinois: InterVarsity Press, 1995), 173.

[20] See James Dunn, Baptism in the Holy Spirit (Philadelphia, Pennsylvania: Westminster Press, 1970), and Gerald Bray, *Romans, the Ancient Christian Commentary on Scripture* (Downers Grove, Illinois: InterVarsity Press, 1998).

[21] If we come to a proper understanding of the normative role of baptism being the time for the reception of the Holy Spirit, we will need

to gain a big-picture perspective on water and Spirit baptism in Acts. Several biblical truths must come together by way of synthesis. I (Bobby) am indebted to Richard Oster, my New Testament professor at Harding University Graduate School, and I. Howard Marshall, The *Acts of the Apostles*, for the following paradigm, which helps us to understand "the exceptions to water and Spirit baptism in Acts."

First, Acts 1:4-8 picks up on the ending of Luke (24:45-49) and lays down the grid for the book of Acts: the witness of the Apostles in the power of the Spirit in Jerusalem, Judea, and Samaria, and to the ends of the world (i.e., the Roman Empire). The book starts in Jerusalem (1:4) and ends in Rome, which was the center of the Roman Empire, with a statement about Paul's bold preaching (28:31).

Second, given this overall grid, Acts 2:38 is very important to the working out of the response that people make to the testimony of the apostles about Jesus. In Acts 1:4-5, Jesus promised that the baptism in the Spirit would soon come. In Acts 2, the promise was fulfilled, first for the twelve men (2:1-4; and especially 14-15), and then it was offered to all people who wanted to respond to Jesus (2:38). Acts 2:38 is very important because repentance and baptism in the name of Jesus for the forgiveness of sins is a response that is here laid down as a normative pattern or paradigm for all people (as per v. 39, "all who are far off"). Luke explicitly sets up Acts 2:38 as the standard for the rest of the book of Acts.

Third, once we understand this grid, we can see that people first responded to the message of faith by being baptized in the name of Jesus in Jerusalem (2:41). By inference, this same message proceeded throughout the rest of Judea as well (5:16). The next phase of Jesus' promise from 1:8 is to reach Samaria with the gospel. God fulfilled this promise by scattering the church throughout Judea and Samaria (Acts 8:1). But in Acts 8, when the Samaritans heard the good news of the kingdom of God and were baptized in the name of Jesus, they did not receive the baptism of the Holy Spirit (8:12, 15-17). The text seems to imply that this was somewhat unusual (8:16). However, given the grid of Acts 1:4-8, it makes sense: the Samaritans were no longer able to consider themselves as a separate people from the Jewish believers in Jerusalem (John 4); they were now tied in with the Jewish Christians in Jerusalem, most notably through deliberate and miraculous signs associated with the apostles Peter and John. These two men were sent from Jerusalem to help bring about the bestowal of the Spirit. This confirms for all that the message of faith has come to the Samaritans and that they were truly joined with God's people. This is an exception to the pattern, which God brought about for the purpose of drawing attention to the joining of the Samaritan Christians with the Jewish Christians, in fulfillment of passages like Jeremiah 31:31-34, where God had said that the two divisions of the Israelite nation would be brought together in the new covenant.

Fourth, the pattern of Acts 2:38 is assumed in the progress of the book of Acts, as is evidenced in the conversion of the Ethiopian eunuch (8:36, 38) and the conversion of Paul (9:18; 22:16). However, God intervenes in the case of Cornelius, for the purpose of convincing Peter that Gentiles are also now to be included. Once Peter realized what God was showing him, he said, "Can anyone keep these people from being baptized with water? They have received the Holy Spirit just as we have." Peter continued to believe that the two baptisms should be tied together (11:15-17). This case, like the case of the Samaritans, is an unusual case where God deviated from the pattern to show Peter and all of us (15:8) that this new people group is also included in the faith and testimony of the new covenant.

Fifth, the pattern of Acts 2:38 continues to be assumed after the conversion of Cornelius as it was beforehand. This fact is substantiated by the conversion of Lydia and her household (16:15), the Philippian jailer and his household (16:31-33), and Crispus, his household, and the many Corinthians who "believed and were baptized" (Acts 18:8). However, in Acts 18 and 19, we read about Apollos (who knew the way of the Lord, but who had to be taught about proper baptism) and then the twelve disciples of John who did not have the Holy Spirit. Once again, we have an entirely new group of people. They are not Israelites, Samaritans, or Gentiles; they are followers of John the Baptist. The first sign Paul looks for to determine if these people are Christians is the possession of the Holy Spirit (19:2). This inquiry is naturally the first question because it is the most important sign of a Christian (Eph. 1:13-14; Rom. 8:9). When Paul finds out that they do not have the Spirit, he automatically assumes that their baptism was in error (19:3). It makes sense that Paul would feel this way only if he believed that reception of the Spirit was typically tied with baptism, as it is in Acts 2:38. The solution to the fact that they did not have the Spirit is found through baptism in the name of Jesus. The confirmation comes when, as part of the baptismal ceremony, Paul lays his hand on them and they speak in tongues.

Sixth, the only other discussion of baptism after Acts 19 occurs when Paul retells the story of his conversion in Acts 22:16. This case explicitly confirms the pattern of Acts 2:38. Thus in Acts, and elsewhere in the New Testament, the effectual saving work of God done by the Holy Spirit is promised to those who embrace Jesus by faith in baptism. Thus, we conclude: the reception of the Spirit commonly occurs during water baptism, but exceptions to the principle do exist.

[22] For technical scholarly support of this point, see Bruce Terry's "Baptized in One Spirit," Restoration Quarterly 21 (1978): 193-200, or Moses Lard, "Baptism in One Spirit into One Body," Lard's Quarterly 1 (March, 1864): 271-282.

[23] For more information on how these terms have been applied incorrectly in the Pentecostal and Charismatic movements, consult Fredrick Dale Brunner, A Theology of the Holy Spirit (Grand Rapids, Michigan: Wm. B. Eerdmans Publishing Co., 1970), and John R. Stott, Baptism and Fullness: The Work of the Holy Spirit Today (Downers Grove, Illinois: InterVarsity Press, 1975).

[24] Those who wonder if "water" in this context is a reference to baptism may want to examine Jack Cottrell's book, Baptism: A Biblical Study (Joplin, Missouri: College Press, 1989), 33ff.

[25] See footnote 20 for more information.

[26] The following story and material is taken from the book by Bobby Harrington and Josh Patrick, *The Disciple Makers Handbook* (Grand Rapids, Michigan: Zondervan, 2017).

[27] A child's inherent standing before God (Matt. 19:13-15) and the sanctifying cover of a parent's faith (7:14) are to be trusted as enough to keep children safe until they reach the necessary level of spiritual development, where they can make the personal decision to turn away from sin (even as a future life path) to faith in Christ.

[28] See F. LaGard Smith, Baptism: *The Believer's Wedding Ceremony* (Cincinnati, Ohio: Standard Publishing, 1989), 115-116. See also Larry Stalley, Baptism In The Early Post-Apostolic Church (M. A. R. Guided Research, Harding University Graduate School, 1980); Jack P. Lewis, "*Baptismal Practices of the Second and Third Century Church,*" Restoration Quarterly vol. 26 (1983): 1-17; and Everett Ferguson, *The Early Christians Speak* (Abilene, Texas: ACU Press, reprint 1994). Attempts to find infant baptism within the description of households coming to faith typically minimizes the fact that "households" in the ancient world typically included relatives, in-laws, and slaves. A careful examination of the conversions in Acts 10 demonstrates this truth.

[29] Kenneth J. Stewart, *In Search of Ancient Roots: The Christian Past and the Evangelical Identity Crisis* (Downers Grove, Illinois: InterVarsity Press, 2017), 128-140.

[30] For more information see Walter Bauer, *A Greek-English Lexicon of the New Testament and Other Early Christian Literature.* 2nd. ed., revised by William Arndt and F. Wilbur Gingrich (Chicago, Illinois: University of Chicago Press, 1979). Also, consult the comprehensive study of Thomas Conant, *The Meaning and Use of Baptizein* (Grand Rapids, Michigan: Kregel Publications, 1977).

[31] In the Septuagint (a Greek translation of the Old Testament) translation of Leviticus 14:15, each of these words is used to indicate the three distinct actions: pouring, sprinkling and dipping.

[32] The first instance of pouring is found in the Didache, written about 20 years after the last book of the New Testament. Pouring is referred to as the third and last method of baptism to resort to if one wants to be baptized. Widespread acceptance of something less than immersion did not occur until the fifth century. See F. LaGard Smith, *Baptism: The Believer's Wedding Ceremony* (Cincinnati, Ohio: Standard Publishing, 1989), 96. See also Larry Stalley, *Baptism In The Early Post-Apostolic Church* (M. A. R. Guided Research, Harding University Graduate School, 1980); Jack P. Lewis, Baptismal Practices of the Second and Third Century Church, *Restoration Quarterly* vol. 26 (1983): 1-17; and Everett Ferguson, *The Early Christians Speak* (Abilene, Texas: ACU Press, reprint 1994).

[33] Consider three further lines of related evidence. First, when a person wanted to be baptized in the New Testament, they went to the water. The Bible never recorded that water was brought to the person seeking baptism. People went to where there was an abundant supply of water ("much water"; see John 3:23; Acts 8:36). This would be necessary only if baptism was by

immersion. Second, the Bible teaches that when people arrived at a place of water, they went *down into it*. The Scriptures indicate that the person being baptized and the person doing the baptism both went down into the water (Acts 8:36; Matt. 3:5-6). Third, after baptism, both the person being baptized and the person performing the baptism came up out of the water (Mark 1:10; Acts 8:39). For people to go down into the water– perform the baptism in the water–and then come out of the water, it only makes sense that baptism was practiced by immersion. All of this would have been needless effort if baptism were by sprinkling or pouring.

[34] David Fletcher, editor, *Baptism and the Remission of Sins: An Historical Perspective* (Joplin, Missouri: College Press, 1990).

[35] Paul Chitwood, *The Sinner's Prayer: An Historical and Theological Analysis* (Ph.D. Dissertation, Southern Baptist Theological Seminary, 2001).

[36] There are no examples from all of the conversions in the book of Acts of anyone asking Jesus into their heart or saying the sinner's prayer. Instead, baptism takes on this role. The practice of baptism in Acts is supported by the theology of the rest of the New Testament and the practice of the ancient church (as reflected in the Nicene Creed). In the typical evangelical presentations and booklets, Scriptures are stretched so they look like they provide scriptural support for the sinner's prayer, but these passages offer weak support at best. Revelation 3:20 says, "If anyone hears my voice and opens the door, I will come in…" This passage was written to the church of Laodicea–people who were already Christians. It is telling people who are already believers about repentance and turning back to the Lord. There is nothing in the context of Revelation 3 about how to become a Christian. John 1:12 states, "To all who received him, to those who believed in his name, he gave the right to become children of God." Once again, there is nothing here about the method God prescribed for expressing your faith to become a child of God. How a person receives Christ is not discussed. In reading ahead to John 3, one learns more about becoming a Christian, but the present passage (John 1:12) does not say how to receive Christ or how to become a Christian. To assume this is what the passage is talking about is to read into Scripture a foreign concept. The impact would be better and more biblical if the sinner's prayer (if it takes on the role of confession in Romans 10:9) led to, or were coupled with, the full response of baptism. It's like a spirit without a body or a marriage vow without a wedding ceremony. God has given baptism to make this covenant commitment concrete, just as he made his covenants concrete in the Old Testament.

[37] The material that follows is taken from John Mark Hicks and Greg Taylor, *Down in the River to Pray: Revisioning Baptism as God's Transforming Work* (Siloam Springs, Arkansas: Leafwood Publishers, 2004).

[38] Everett Ferguson, *Baptism in the Early Church: History, Theology, and Liturgy in the First Five Centuries* (Grand Rapids, Michigan: Wm. B. Eerdmans Publishing Co., 2009); see also his *The Early Christians Speak* (Abilene, Texas: ACU Press, reprint 1994).

[39] To hold that God will not save the un-immersed, one would have to minimize some of the central elements of biblical teaching and the work of God's Spirit: a) one must diminish personal faith as the central and essential human response to God's Grace (John 3:16; Rom. 3:25; Rom. 10:9-10; Eph. 2:8-9). Although important, we believe that baptism is not on the same level; it is a secondary matter of God-given methodology for the purpose of expressing this faith. The Bible repeatedly teaches that salvation is by *grace through faith*; b) one must minimize the biblical teaching that God looks at the heart to see what is most fundamental and essential in our motivations as we respond to his grace (1 Sam. 16: 8; Acts 15:7-8). We believe God weighs the motives of the heart and central intentions as being more important than external religious ordinances, although both are important (Matt. 23:23; Mark 2: 23-28; etc.); c) one must discount the biblical teaching on the nature and work of the indwelling Holy Spirit of God. One must advocate that countless millions of devoted, but un-immersed followers of Christ throughout history have been deceived in their belief that the Spirit of God has indwelt and sealed them as his own. One must also hold that the majority of Christ's followers in the present have also been deceived about the Spirit's work in their lives and about their relationship with God through him. It would mean the majority of Christ's followers at present and in history are lost. This horrifying view not only appears to deny God's promises, but also calls into question God's goodness and providence; and d) one must put undue emphasis and weight on the act of baptism. This would cause people to rely upon their baptism, something they have done, as opposed to a complete reliance on Christ's blood.

[40] Robert Fife, "Why Must I Be Baptized," from an address delivered to the North American Christian Convention in Atlanta, Georgia, on July 11, 1984.

[41] There is the biblical example of the Spirit coming to people who did not follow the proper form of a certain religious rite. Eldad and Medad did not appear with the other elders before God as prescribed, but God sent his Spirit upon them anyway (Num. 11:24-30). Later, Hezekiah stirred a religious revival. He called the people to come to Jerusalem to celebrate the Passover, even though it could not be done properly. First, no one was ceremonially clean and prepared to take it. Second, they had to take it one month later than prescribed. Hezekiah prayed for the people. He said, "May the Lord, who is good, pardon everyone who sets his heart on seeking God—the Lord, the God of his fathers—even if he is not clean according to the rules of the sanctuary." The Bible says, "And the Lord heard Hezekiah" (2 Chron. 30: 18-20). And one must not forget Cornelius, who received the Holy Spirit before his baptism (Acts 10).

[42] It is important not to confuse the form of the response (baptism) and the substance of the response (faith). Both are not equal or essential. The substance is the essential element.

[43] Barton Stone stressed this point to the more legalistic people in the Restoration Movement. See Leonard Allen's chapter entitled, "Who Is a Christian," in *Distant Voices* (Abilene, Texas: ACU Press, 1993).

[44] Although they are closely related in the Bible, the indwelling Holy Spirit, not water baptism, is the essential mark of salvation. Ephesians 1:13-14, "And now you also have heard the truth, the good news that God saves you. *And when you believed in Christ, he identified you as his own by giving you the Holy Spirit*, whom he promised long ago. *The Spirit is God's guarantee that he will give us everything he promised* and that he has purchased us to be his own people. This is just one more reason for us to praise our glorious God" (NLT). Romans 8:9, "But you are not controlled by your sinful nature. You are controlled by the Spirit if you have the Spirit of God living in you. *And remember that those who do not have the Spirit of Christ living in them are not Christians at all*" (NLT). See also 2 Cor. 1: 21-22; 1 John 3:24; 4:13. Biblical scholar Gordon Fee puts it this way: "For Paul the reception of the Spirit is the *sine qua non* of Christian life. The Spirit is what essentially distinguishes believer from nonbeliever; the Spirit is what especially marks the beginning of Christian life (Gal. 3: 2-5); the Spirit above all is what makes a person a child of God. For Paul therefore to 'get saved' means first of all to 'receive the Spirit,'" *God's Empowering Presence* (Peabody, Massachusetts: Hendrickson Publishers, 1994), 178, 855. It's helpful to summarize the work of God's indwelling Spirit so we can assess whether or not it truly dwells within. It is surely wisest to look at a composite picture of the indwelling work of the Spirit, not just to focus on one aspect. There are at least eight elements that result from the Holy Spirit's inward ministry: a) God's indwelling Spirit enables people to grasp and embrace the core truth of the cross (1 Cor. 2: 12-15 & 1 Jn. 2: 20-27); b) God's indwelling Spirit inspires people to say with personal commitment: "Jesus is Lord" (1 Cor. 12:3; 1 John 4:1-3); c) God's indwelling Spirit witnesses in the inner being that a person is truly God's child (Rom. 8); d) "For all who are led by the Spirit of God are children of God. So you should not be like cowering, fearful slaves. You should behave instead like God's very own children, adopted into his family—calling him 'Father, dear Father.' For his Holy Spirit speaks to us deep in our hearts and tells us that we are God's children" (Romans 8:14-16, NLT). For the historical and ecumenical consensus in support of our position, see Thomas C. Oden, *Life In The Spirit* Systematic *Theology*: Volume Three (San Francisco, California: Harper Collins, 1992), 170ff. The un-immersed and great Christian leader John Wesley described it this way: "By the 'testimony of the Spirit' I mean an inward impression of the soul, whereby the Spirit of God immediately and directly witnesses to my spirit that I am a child of God, that 'Jesus Christ hath loved me and given himself for me,' that all my sins are blotted out, and I, even I, am reconciled to God. John Wesley, *The Works of John Wesley*, Albert C. Outler, ed. (Nashville, Tennessee: Abingdon, 1984), 1: 287; e) God's indwelling Spirit leads people to dwell upon Christ (Eph. 4:16-18); f) God's indwelling Spirit leads people into a righteous moral lifestyle (Rom. 8:9-17; Gal. 5:16-26); g) God's indwelling Spirit prompts inner joy, peace, and hope through faith in Christ. (Rom. 14:17; 15:13); h) God's indwelling Spirit gives people unique abilities for ministry in the church (Rom. 12:3-8; 1 Cor. 12: 8-29; 1 Pet. 4; 10-11); i) Most significantly, God's indwelling Spirit produces the fruit of true Christlikeness: 2 Corinthians 3:18 (NLT), "And as the Spirit of the Lord

works within us, we become more and more like him and reflect his glory," and Galatians 5:22-25 (NLT): "But when the Holy Spirit controls our lives, he will produce this kind of fruit in us: love, joy, peace, patience, kindness, goodness, faithfulness, gentleness, and self-control." When we see such evidence, we can be sure that it was not produced by mere human effort. And it is not produced by Satan, for he is not in the business of humbling us before God, drawing us to Christ, softening our hearts continuously before God, and enabling us to become like Christ and love as he did.

[45] Even in the Stone-Campbell Movement, where baptism became a central ordinance to be restored, its early leaders wisely acknowledged that God's saving power is not limited to baptism. Alexander Campbell emphatically stressed this point to the people of a legalistic bent in the Restoration Movement, see "Lunenburg Correspondence," *Millennial Harbinger*, July 8, 1837. It was recognition of the indwelling presence of the Holy Spirit that convinced Peter and the Jerusalem council that God had accepted Cornelius and his household, even before they had been baptized. Peter stated the matter this way: "God, who knows the heart, showed that he accepted them by giving the Holy Spirit to them, just as he did to us. He made no distinction between us and them, *for he purified their hearts by faith*" (Acts 15:8-9). Thus, there are three essential qualities I look for before we can personally think that someone who has not experienced a biblical baptism might be a Christian, while recognizing that, in the end, it is a matter of personal opinion: a) a genuine, repentant faith in Jesus Christ; b) the clear testimony about the work of the indwelling Holy Spirit, including an ongoing love for Jesus Christ; and c) the objective fruit of the Holy Spirit transforming one's life into the likeness of Christ.

[46] R. T. France, *The Gospel of Matthew*, The New International Commentary on the New Testament (Grand Rapids, Michigan: Eerdmans, 2007).

[47] See H. Bietenhard, "Prepositions with Baptizo," in *The International Dictionary of New Testament Theology*, edited by Colin Brown (Grand Rapids, Michigan: Zondervan Publishing Company, 1975), 3: 1207 - 1211; Lars Hartman, "Into the Name of Jesus, " *New Testament Studies* 20 (1973): 432-440; and Lars Hartman, "Baptism Into the Name of Jesus' and Early Christianity," *Studia Theologica* 28 (1974): 21-48.

[48] We often see ourselves as approaching this matter in a similar way to what Peter did in Acts 10. We may personally believe that God has given his Spirit and salvation, somehow, apart from baptism. This is exactly what Peter faced (Acts 10:44-48; 15:7-9). Peter rejoiced, but he still insisted that Cornelius and his household be baptized in water because this was the full response God wanted: "Then Peter said, 'Can anyone keep these people from being baptized with water? They have received the Holy Spirit just as we have.' So he ordered that they be baptized in the name of Jesus Christ" (Acts 10:47-48). Similarly, we rejoice in the presence of personal faith and the apparent indwelling Holy Spirit in the lives of many Christ followers, but we also encourage them to follow through with biblical baptism. For us, this practice is an important doctrine.

[49] As one would expect, Roman Catholic and all Orthodox churches require official church baptism before one is recognized as a formal member of the church. But the vast majority of Protestant churches also require baptism before formal membership can be recognized: Southern Baptists and Christian Churches (among others) require immersion, and the Presbyterian Church of America and United Methodist Churches (among others) require baptism by sprinkling, pouring, or immersion.